Georgian Trick Riders in
American Wild West Shows,
1890s–1920s

Georgian Trick Riders in American Wild West Shows, 1890s–1920s

Irakli Makharadze

McFarland & Company, Inc., Publishers
Jefferson, North Carolina

This book is a revised and expanded version of *Wild West Georgians* by Irakli Makharadze and Akaki Chkhaidze (Tbilisi, Georgia: New Media Tbilisi, 2002). It was translated into English by Salome and Nino Makharadze.

All photographs are from the collection of Irakli Makharadze except as noted.

LIBRARY OF CONGRESS CATALOGUING-IN-PUBLICATION DATA

Makharadze, Irakli.
    Georgian trick riders in American wild west shows, 1890s–1920s / Irakli Makharadze.
        p.   cm.
    Includes bibliographical references and index.

    ISBN 978-0-7864-9739-3 (softcover : acid free paper) ∞
    ISBN 978-1-4766-1880-7 (ebook)

    1. Rodeo performers—United States. 2. Trick riding.
3. Wild west shows—United States 4. Georgian Americans.
5. Georgians (South Caucasians)—United States. I. Title.
GV1833.5.M34 2015
791.8′40973—dc23   2015006103

BRITISH LIBRARY CATALOGUING DATA ARE AVAILABLE

© 2015 Irakli Makharadze. All rights reserved

No part of this book may be reproduced or transmitted in any form or by any means, electronic or mechanical, including photocopying or recording, or by any information storage and retrieval system, without permission in writing from the publisher.

Cover image (ca. 1898) of Georgian horsemen is from the author's collection

Printed in the United States of America

McFarland & Company, Inc., Publishers
    Box 611, Jefferson, North Carolina 28640
        www.mcfarlandpub.com

Dedicated to my dear
family—Nana, Salome and Nino

What good will money bring to a man,
He has to have a good horse!
          —Vaja Pshavela (1862–1915), Georgian poet.

There never was a horse that couldn't be rode;
There never was a rider that couldn't be throwed.
                                —Old cowboy saying.

Table of Contents

Introduction	1
1. Georgia—the Land of Wine and the Golden Fleece	17
2. Guria: The Heart of Georgia	24
3. From East to West	28
4. Down in Albion: The Russians Are Coming!	40
5. On Her Majesty's Service	47
6. The Georgian Cossacks	54
7. Master of the Rough Riders	63
8. Alexis Gogokhia/Georgian	79
9. Coming to America	83
10. Promised Land	92
11. All Born Princes: Daredevils	105
12. *Who's Guilty?*	128
13. Gurian Republic and the Outlaw-Pirals	132
14. Life and Times of the Wild West	143
15. The Death Race	155
16. Prince Luka: Russia's Famous Player	165
17. The Georgian Amazons	174
18. This Is the End	189
Chapter Notes	195
Bibliography	203
Index	205

Introduction

In the beginning of the 1970s, as a little boy aged 12 to 13, I discovered Western movies, which consequently became a true passion of my life. The Western genre, with its vast, open plains, towering mountains of the Wild West, lone riders and "redskin" Indians, highly attracted the Soviet audience, especially Georgian spectators. The very first Western I saw was *The Bad Man of Brimstone*, with Wallace Beery. During that period, Tbilisi, the capital of Georgia, had a movie theater that ran so-called "trophy" films, black and white, mostly American. Allegedly, they were taken from Europe during World War II, but I still wonder about the origin of the name, since the United States and the Soviet Union were allies during the war. Also I saw some Ken Maynard and Buck Jones movies and, of course, *Stagecoach* (titled as *The Journey Will Be Dangerous*), by the great John Ford. John Wayne became a real idol for people of many different nationalities, different social backgrounds, and drastically different living environments. John Wayne's name has become a symbol of faithfulness, courage, and infinite love for one's homeland. That is exactly why Wayne was a favorite hero for Georgians as well. Despite the fact that the Soviet government continuously criticized and chastised Wayne, calling him a reactionary, a militarist, and an anti–Communist, Wayne's popularity was not harmed at all. There were people in the former Soviet Georgia who had never seen any of his movies. They had only seen his photos or had heard about him from radio station "Freedom," which was banned at that time. Some people went as far as giving their children the first name of John, very uncommon in Georgia. My compatriot, U.S. Army General John Shalikashvili, improved his English with the help of Wayne's movies. According to Shalikashvili: "I spoke a little bit [of English]. But not much beyond 'yes' and 'no' and 'what time is it.' And the stories that subsequently have been told that I learned English by watching John Wayne movies is only a little bit of a stretch ... I would run to the local movie theater. There I would sit through movies in order to learn English. In those days movies didn't

Introduction

start at a specific time and end at a specific time, but they would roll continuously.... The first time through, it wouldn't make much sense to me. But the second time through, it would begin to make a little more sense. Now in my memory, which is probably very faulty, a lot of those movies were John Wayne movies or at least were Wild West movies."[1]

> It may sound strange, but there is an interesting connection between the Soviet dictator and master of one-sixth of the world, Joseph Stalin, and the Western, a purely American phenomenon. Joseph Jugashvili a.k.a. Stalin was born in town of Gori, Georgia, the homeland of well-known revolutionaries and terrorists, and began his career as a mastermind of bank robberies to finance the Bolshevik party. The most famous one took place on June 25, 1907, when Stalin's daredevil "combat team" robbed carriages of the State Bank in the center of Tbilisi, killed six men, and stole 250,000 rubles. Afterwards he was trying hard to hide his past, eliminating his old comrades, friends, witnesses, and documents, but he wasn't able to bury all truth. Apropos of this, President Franklin Roosevelt once remarked that although he had expected the head of the Soviet government to be a gentleman, he found in the Kremlin a former Caucasian bandit.[2]

According to Nikita Khrushchev, Stalin liked cowboy movies and was dissatisfied that Soviet film industry didn't have homegrown Westerns to admire. Sometimes he used to curse Westerns and give them their proper ideological evaluation, but then immediately order new ones. His favorites were John Ford and John Wayne. But in spite of his

Gurian trick riders, 1892, London.

Introduction

enjoyment of the films, as British film critic Michael Munn wrote in the book *John Wayne: The Man Behind the Myth* (2004), Stalin once declared at the end of a showing that Wayne, a determined anti–Communist, was a threat to the cause and should be assassinated. Assassins were supposedly sent to Los Angeles but failed to kill Wayne before Stalin's death. When Khrushchev met John Wayne in 1959, he told him, "That was the decision of Stalin in his last mad years. I rescinded the order."

In the 60s and 70s, Soviet audiences were given an opportunity to see more American movies. But we were never spoiled by good American Westerns; we were left with no other choice but to watch so-called "Westerns" made in East Germany, Romania, and Yugoslavia, which gained popularity with Soviet audiences. In fact, one of the movies, *The Trail of a Falcon*, was partly made in Georgia. This movie was my first encounter with the "Native American Indians" personified by various Georgian and foreign actors. Although the makers of these films attempted to imitate Western movies, what they really achieved was an extremely meek resemblance of them. One of the movies that gained the Soviet audiences' great attention was *The Magnificent Seven*, which was released after Nikita Khrushchev briefly lifted censorship in the early 60s. None of the previously released movies, with the exception of the *Tarzan* films with Johnny Weissmuller, had ticket office lines of the same length as *The Magnificent Seven*. The number of spectators did not decrease even on the reruns of the film, or even a couple of years after its release, when the audience had seen *The Magnificent Seven* many times. A total of 67 million people saw *The Magnificent Seven* in the USSR, compared to 7 million in France.

During these times, the business of speculators—illegal sellers who would sell the tickets for a much higher price—flourished. But no one cared for money when there was such a spectacular event to look forward to. Every time a movie was shown on screen, the audience would become part of the action on the screen. Some would cheer the film characters or repeat the lines by heart in Russian, since the movies were translated into the Russian language. Coming out of the show, the audience would rush to buy the black and white photos sold on the street, produced by taking a photo of the movie on the screen. At that time, such a photo would normally cost 20 Soviet kopeks. On the black market, one U.S. dollar equaled three rubles; there were 100 kopeks in a ruble.

Introduction

Among the film's characters, Chris (played by Yul Brynner) achieved a real cult following in the Soviet Union. Shaved heads became the high fashion of the day. People imitated Yul Brynner's movements; everybody admired his self-restraint and calmness. Another audience favorite was taciturn Britt (played by James Coburn). Boys would compete in knife-throwing for hours. Steve McQueen was the one I admired most. His ironic and courageous Vin overshadowed everybody else in the movie. I have repeated his line, "You know, I've been in some towns where the girls weren't very pretty. Matter of fact, I've been in some towns where they were downright ugly. But this is the first time I've ever been in a town where there are no girls at all—except little ones." These lines became famous, but in Russian, since the Soviet Union restricted screenings in original versions and of course restricted dubbing in any other language than Russian.

After seeing the film, people desperately wanted to wear jeans, which were not produced in the Soviet Union but were sneaked in the country, mainly by Soviet diplomats, sailors, tourists, and others, and sold on the black market. Jeans were very expensive. They sold for anywhere from 150 to 250 rubles. As a reference point, an average monthly salary was under 150 rubles.

Nevertheless, one of the movies that fascinated me more than others was William Wellman's *Buffalo Bill* (1944), with Joel McCrea as Buffalo Bill Cody and beautiful Maureen O'Hara as his wife. From then on, I had a deep interest in the Wild West and Western movie history. But we lived behind the Iron Curtain in the big cage, where all the Western values were strongly prohibited. Happily, times have changed.

Once in 1992, an article about Apache warrior Geronimo in *National Geographic* triggered my interest in the history of Georgian trick riders, mistakenly labeled as Russian Cossacks,[3] who performed in Buffalo Bill's Wild West and other American shows during the end of the 19th and beginning of the 20th centuries. When I saw the Pawnee Bill's Historic Wild West poster with Geronimo in the center and a portrait of Prince Luka, a Cossack, on the left, I wanted to find out more about this man, whose name was Luka Chkhartishvili. It took me several months to find out who that guy was, and when at last I succeeded, I knew instantly that I had not only a film subject but a book subject, too. That guy was Georgian, and he was the head of one of the main attractions in the show, the

Introduction

Left to right: Konstantine Chkhartishvili, Luka Chkhartishvili, and Nikoloz Surguladze, 1898.

Introduction

so-called "Russian Cossack" riders, performing with the most popular American shows, especially Buffalo Bill Cody's Wild West.

In general, the Cossacks lived in Russia. (The "Cossack" in Russian is spelled "Kazak.") They served in the military and defended the Russian borders from enemy assault. Despite their notorious reputation for holding demonstrations and for terrorizing the Jews and other nations of Russian Empire, including Georgians, the Cossacks became very successful and were known as the "Russian cowboys" thanks to Buffalo Bill Cody.

It took me more months to find out that there were no Cossacks involved in the American shows, but that all of them were riders from the western part of Georgia known as Guria. Gurians are ethnic Georgians who speak a local dialect of the Georgian language. I had known about Gurian-Georgian riders from my childhood. I am Gurian, too, but was born and raised in Tbilisi. When I would visit my father's village in Guria, I sometimes heard the stories about trick riders told by old

Georgian horsemen, circa 1912.

6

villagers. "Gurians made the crowds in America go wild, but they were already wild back home," they would say. Subsequently, as I discovered, it was confirmed by numerous articles in American and European newspapers and magazines, which stated that "The Cossacks'" exhibition of riding "must be seen to be believed." Here are some examples: "The rough riding of the Cossacks surpassed anything we have ever seen. These daredevils dashed around the tent at breakneck speed and rode their steeds in all positions—on back, belly, side and rump—at times trailing a hand or foot upon the ground and seemingly endangering life and limb. One of them rode around the tent standing on his horse with his boots on."[4] Or, "The troupe of Imperial Russian Cossacks were a feature that pleased. Their riding was simply perfect, and some of the stunts that they performed while their horses were rushing around the ring at full speed fairly made one hold his breath."[5]

For a variety of reasons, the Gurian trick riders were referred as "Russian Cossacks." The most important reason was the fact that Georgia was part of the Russian Empire at that time, and so each Georgian was referred to as Russian. Georgia was annexed by the Czar's Russia in 1801 and by Soviet Russia in 1921, and they had a chance to made it third time in 2008, but failed.

American author and journalist William E. Curtis, who visited Georgia in 1910, in his book *Around the Black Sea* accurately depicted the situation in the country:

> The political situation here is practically the same as that in Poland. Georgia is a conquered province. It was added to the Russian empire without the consent of the people. They are Russian subjects by compulsion and they do not like it. Their former king appealed to the Russians for protection against the Persians more than a century ago; the Russians responded to the appeal and have "assimilated" the kingdom of Georgia as they did the kingdom of Poland.[6]

From the historical view, the Georgian-Russian relations embrace a short period of time but this period is burdened with bloodshed and tragic and dramatic events. The Georgian nation was tired and exhausted from incessant and bloody wars against the Islamic states. After the Middle Ages, Georgia was heading towards a single, united state ideal. To fulfill this ideal, it was necessary to get rid of external enemies, to remove them, which Georgia failed to do due to its own geopolitical location

Introduction

Left to right: **Konstantine Chkhartishvili, Teimuraz Chkhartishvili, Kaisar Kvitaishvili, Onophre Tsuladze (?), Platon Murvanidze, Massachusetts, circa 1908.**

and other objective reasons. Outside enemies broke up and separated Georgia into parts and did their best to fully destroy and demolish the Georgian nation and the Georgian state. The bloodshedding struggles between the principalities (i.e. between Georgians) exhausted Georgia's limited forces, which was profitable for its enemies. In the second half of the 18th century, King Irakli II saw vividly that three great rival states—Iran, Turkey and Russia—were putting forward claims for dominating in the Transcaucasia. Georgia was troubled by all three of them. The state had to make its choice: either the Islamic world, or Russia, through which King Irakli hoped to transform the state structures and life by means of the progressive or European way. Georgia was finally torn off (figuratively) the way leading to Europe, after the fall of Constantinople. To be with Russia, in the opinion of many Georgians, gave a chance to Georgia to break through this blockade, to retrieve its seized territories, to restore the broken link with Europe, through Russia, and to enter the European family this way. As a result of this, on 24 July 1783

Introduction

the Georgievski Treaty was concluded, which is differently evaluated by the historians of different generations. However, this treaty in no way implied the abolishment of the statehood of Georgia and its transformation into an absolute gubernia (province, in the Russian language) of Russia, with all its unwelcome consequences. The Georgian kings and nobles, diplomats, and ordinary people sincerely trusted Russia—as it was also of Orthodox belief—and still considered the Islamic world to be their main enemy. Russia made use of this for its own benefit and always used Georgia for its own political intentions and goals.

The above-mentioned William E. Curtis wrote:

> There is no loyalty to the tzar and nothing to inspire it. The administration of the Caucasus is purely military. The first thought in the Russian mind is contest. After that there is no other thought but to retain possession. Instead of planting trees and encouraging the people to improve their method of agriculture, the Russians build fortresses, and instead of building schoolhouses they build barracks. The railway across the province and that which runs down to the Persian border were primarily for the movement of troops,

Georgian trick riders at Grant's Tomb, New York, 1908 (courtesy Buffalo Bill Museum and Grave, Golden, Colorado).

Introduction

and military supplies are given preference over all freight. The famous road through the Caucasus Mountains is for military purposes rather than for commerce. At least one hundred and fifty thousand soldiers are kept on a war footing in this province alone. That number of men are not only withdrawn from the fields and factories, and the number of producers reduced, but the peasants who work the farms, the shopkeepers and other peaceful members of the population, are taxed to pay for their support, which is a continual grievance that cannot be removed. If the money that is spent upon military purposes could be devoted to material development and the education of the people, the army would not be needed.[7]

There is no doubt no that those so-called "Cossacks" were Georgians, because in almost every case the surnames of these horsemen ended with suffixes "-dze," "-shvili," and "-ia," which are typically ethnic Georgian names.

I followed my discovery, and pretty soon I was all over the archives in Georgia and abroad (mostly in the U.S.) to find out more about those mysterious people, including extensive traveling in Georgia. I even put an advertisement in local newspapers and asking people to contact me if they had any kind of materials regarding the riders. From time to time I visited Lanchkhuti, about 300 km from Tbilisi, which is a hometown of many of these riders. Like a door-to-door salesman, I asked for photos and materials and luckily discovered photographs in homes. Even though my country has been separated from the Soviet Union for years, many people were still reluctant to get the photos out of fear of some type of political reprisal.

With the help of my website, www.georgians.ge, and my page on Facebook, I got acquainted with some Wild West show experts: American Richard Alexis Georgian—his grandfather was famous "Cossack" horseman Alexis Gogokhia-Georgian—Steve Friesen, the director of Buffalo Bill Museum & Grave, Golden, Colorado, and Tom F. Cunningham and Alan Gallop from Great Britain. We exchanged materials, photos etc. In 2008, I was invited by Steve Friesen to conduct research about the Georgian trick riders. Mr. Friesen very graciously invited me to stay at his home. Mr. and Mrs. Friesen were wonderful hosts, and I had a delightful time staying at their household. Overall, my visit turned out to be very productive. I was able to find important new materials (photos, newspapers, articles, etc.) at his museum.

Four or five years ago, I received an email from a man named Aron

Introduction

Nuttal, which stated: "My name is Aron! A few years ago my mother told me that one of my ancestors rode with Buffalo Bill. I was intrigued to find out who he was! A few years passed and I had no lead. The only thing we knew was that he wasn't American and that he was from somewhere near Russia. I searched and searched and nearly gave up until I was searching a website which had Russian Cossacks on. When I looked at the bottom of the page I saw a familiar-looking figure, almost the spitting image of my great-grandfather. They had labeled him as Ivan Makorazdze. This didn't help, as there was no record of him anywhere, until I found your website and saw him and his proper name, Luka Chkhartishvili. He looks so much like my great-grandfather, who unfortunately has his mother's name, which is Lyons. His full name was Roland Lyons, and a captain (I think in the First World War). I know you may have no record of this or maybe you have, due to the rough riders having to destroy a lot of their documents. Please, if you know anything, it would fill a great big hole in my life and my mother's also. It has been very frustrating at times, but I never give up, and I thank God for leading me this far...." He also sent the picture of Luka taken at the Chicago World's Fair, 1893, which was labeled as Ivane Makharadze.

Luka Chkhartishvili, circa end of the 19th century.

The story of Luka was not uncommon, as many of the Georgian riders had settled in the U.S. and assumed new identities. As it turned out, some Georgians along with Luka (Nikoloz Surguladze, Luka Ebralidze, etc.) even became bigamists. They had two families: one in America and one in Georgia. As the story of Nikoloz Surguladze, one of the "Cossacks," goes, when he returned home to Georgia, he brought

Introduction

his American child's photos and even film. Enraged, his Georgian wife burned it all.

Every Saturday and Sunday, I was spending my time visiting so-called Dry Bridge market in Tbilisi, where you can find everything from vintage clothing, original artwork, and antiques to Lenin and Stalin posters, Soviet memorabilia, and handmade jewelry. I was looking for riders' photos, and I got lucky: I found three pictures of them. Two photos I've purchased, and one I exchanged for a postcard of Old Tbilisi (I had a pretty good collection of pre-revolutionary postcards of Tbilisi).

Once, one acquaintance of mine, who is a collector of traditional Georgian dress and weapons, called me. "One guy is selling a photo of a Gurian rider," he said. "How much?" I asked him. "I don't know, but I'll check it for you. OK?"

One week later I received the call from him: "Come to my place," he said, "and look at the photo." I rushed over immediately, and after 20 minutes, I was in his place and held the picture in my hand—George Georgian (his real last name is unknown) from Bud Atkinson's American Circus and Wild West Show. It was a beautiful photograph and in very

George Georgian in fur hat, driver is unknown, Bud Atkinson's American Circus and Wild West Show, circa 1912.

Introduction

good condition. "How much?" I asked him. "Nothing," he replied. "What do you mean, nothing?" "It's present from me," he grinned. "We are very much alike. I like such fanatics as you are.... So, go ahead, enrich your collection."

Frankly, I was very happy, and very surprised.

Slowly, I collected scores of pictures and began piecing together the story of the Georgian trick riders. I was very lucky with my research, since the following year, to the best of my knowledge, I had almost all available materials about the Georgians in the American Wild West shows. That's how the documentary *Riders of the Wild West* came to exist. I made it in 1997, followed by a book, *Riders of the Wild West*, about the lives and American adventures of those Georgian riders. It turned out to be a big success in Georgia. The documentary was shown by almost every local TV channel and was chosen as the finalist at the Flagstaff International Film Festival, Flagstaff, AZ. I was on cloud nine but totally unaware of the fact that it was just the tip of an iceberg, for when the riders' remaining relatives living in Georgia saw and heard about the film they literally flooded me with more material. That's how I bumped into my second discovery. This was just a beginning.

Surviving photographs, programs, and letters document how Georgian riders—"Cossacks" presented themselves in totally different world, with dignity, grace, and confidence. I really love these images. I held several photo exhibitions named Georgian Horsemen in America; the first one took place in Tbilisi, at the Georgian National Open Air Museum

Nikoloz Surguladze.

Introduction

of Ethnography, on June 11, 2005, with the support of the U.S. Embassy, Georgian Glass & Mineral Water, and the Georgian National Museum. The celebration opened with two horseback riders dressed in Georgian and American cowboy outfits cutting a red ribbon. Gurian folk singers, American country music, dancing, games, and food entertained young and old alike. "Wild West" T-shirts, coffee mugs, and pins were sold to raise money for future programs at the Georgian National Museum. Local and national media covered the event. In April 2011, the exhibition, called *Photo Narrative: Georgians in American History*, was held in The Harriman Institute at Columbia University, New York.

I went on with my researches, enriching my personal archive with some unique material. The riders' relatives living in the U.S. were incredibly supportive (and still are) of the project, as well as the Garlow Fellowship that was granted to me by the Buffalo Bill Historical Center (now Buffalo Bill Center of the West), Cody, Wyoming, and my research in Buffalo Bill Museum & Grave in Golden, Colorado.

An unknown rider.

Bill McCall, a Cody native who has worked as a business consultant in my country for more than a decade, helped me to connect with the museum in Cody and foster the "sister city" relationship between Cody and Lanchkhuti. When I came to Cody and showed the photos of Georgians, Robert Shimp, then the executive director of the museum, said to the reporter from the *Cody Enterprise*: "This is something we haven't known before." The curator of the Buffalo Bill Museum, Juti Winchester, added: "He has photos we've never seen. For more than 100 years, no one had had known the nationality of the riders. They were the real McCoy." It is one thing to obtain information through books and movies, and it is yet another thing to "touch" the past with your own hands, see with your own eyes the places connected with famous people such as Buffalo Bill Cody, John "Jeremiah Liver Eating" Johnston, or Tom Horn. This experience only increased my passion and interest in the Wild West.

When I returned from Cody, I began to campaign for the Georgian stamp honoring the trick riders. The process took three years, and the stamp was finally issued in late 2006. I selected the design for the commemorative stamp. It was printed by Georgia Post's stamp security printer in a quantity of 15,000.

After almost two decades, my research has taken me deep into the story behind the Georgian trick riders, how they came to be associated with Buffalo Bill in the first place, and what life was like for them while on tour and in the States.

1. Georgia—the Land of Wine and the Golden Fleece

"During the distributing of pieces of the world to all the people of the Earth, the Georgians were having a party and doing some serious drinking. As a result, they arrived late and were told by God that all the land had been shared out. When they replied that they were late only because they had been lifting their glasses in praise of Him, God was pleased and gave the Georgians that part of Earth He had been reserving for Himself." This is the anecdote that every modern Georgian likes to tell foreigners. It's worth mentioning that most authorities agree that Georgia is the birthplace of winemaking. The cultivation of cultural grapes and the wine production from them in the territory of Georgia were developed six thousand years BCE. This is confirmed by seeds found in ancient burials in the territory of Georgia and the archaeological excavations of ancient Georgian settlements, whose age is eight thousand years. On the vessels discovered there frequently are pictured images of the grapevine. Today there are more than 500 aboriginal grape varieties still cultivated in this small country surrounded by the Caucasus Mountains. The art of vine-growing, or viticulture, has been passed from one generation of Georgians to another and is considered an integral part of the Georgian genetic inheritance. Indeed, the Georgian word "ghvino" is thought to be the root of the French "vin" and English "wine."[1]

Georgians are proud of their wines. Here is a quote from the diary of an unknown Gurian rider: "We drank a lot toast today, we drank a lot of whisky and vodka, but nothing compares to our Odessa wine...." Odessa wine is made from the Isabella grape, which is used for juice and wine production. It was brought to Georgia through seaport city Odessa. That's one of the reasons this variety is also called Odessa among Georgians.

Georgia is an ancient country situated to the east of the Black Sea

Georgian Trick Riders in American Wild West Shows

Georgian horsemen, United States, circa 1899.

and surrounded by the Caucasus Mountains in the north. A former republic of the Soviet Union, it shares borders with Russia, Turkey, Armenia, and Azerbaijan. The country occupies about 27,000 square miles (69,700 square kilometers). It has been an Orthodox Christian country since AD 337. The history of the Georgian state, dating back 3000 years, is a never-ending battle for freedom and independence. Wedged between the competing interests of multiple empires—Roman and Byzantine, Ottoman, Persian, Russian, and even the British (depositing 20,000 troops in Georgia in 1919)—the Georgians were forced to fight; they were warriors.

Georgian men, according to English historian David Marshall Lang, are generally tall, handsome men of dark complexion, fearless and renowned for chivalry, skill in battle, and ferocity. Their women are celebrated for beauty and grace and brought high prices at the slave markets for Turkish harems, as did Circassian women.[2] (Circassia is a region in the North Caucasus and along the northeast shore of the Black Sea. The Circassians are Sunnite Muslims.)

It is said that the dog is indeed the best friend of a man, but the horse is what created a civilization. The horse and horsemanship helped to protect various nations from the threat of extinction. Georgians were no exception. From ancient times, those who bred horses were highly respected, and good breeders were always needed and well regarded by the various Georgian kings. Although a lucrative position, it was also politically risky, because breeders were responsible for providing the king with a strong and reliable cavalry. The fact that Georgian ancestors paid special attention to horsemanship is proven by the discovery of horse decorations, the figures of the horse riders, and other objects. According to the archeological data, the horse, as an animal utilized in warfare as well as transportation, entered the lifestyle of the tribes living in the Georgian territory in the late Middle Bronze Age. Horse skeletons were also discovered in ancient burials. As it turns out, the ancient horses had thin legs and small hoofs.

The only surviving epic of the Hellenistic era, *The Argonautika*, by the Greek Apollonius Rhodios, is the tale of Jason and Argonauts, who sailed to Colchis, the ancient part of Western Georgia, in order to obtain the Golden Fleece. The author wrote: "They went on the ship, and sailed toward the field of Ares, situated at the bank of the river, with the view on the entire city.... The Colchis would hold various athletic competitions and horseback riding spectacles here, commemorating their heroes and kings."[3] According to Greek mythology, Colchis was a fabulously wealthy land, where in the sacred grove of the war god Ares, the legendary King Aeetes hung the Golden Fleece until it was seized by Jason and Argonauts. Colchis was also the land where the mythological Prometheus (Amirani in Georgian) was punished by being chained to a Caucasus mountain while an eagle ate his liver for revealing to humanity the secret of fire. It is said that Colchis also the homeland of women warriors—Amazons.

The horse was rarely used in agriculture. The ancient bridle discovered in Georgia also dates back to the late Middle Bronze Age. It was during this time that the process of including horses in burials had started in Georgia. The Tabals, Georgian tribes that lived during the 1st century BCE, were famous for having the best kinds of horses. Georgian kings and statesmen would send horses as very precious gifts to the kings and noblemen of their allies and patron countries. The Georgians paid a special attention to military upbringing as an opportunity of

The Czar's Georgian convoy, by an unknown artist, circa 1860.

developing stamina and courage on the battlefield. Such kind of training started in early childhood.

In AD 141, during the reign of Parsman, King of Iberia (Iberia is located in the eastern part of Georgia), an invitation was extended from Rome to participate in a riding contest in honor of Mars. The king, along with his son Radamist, and a small group of Georgians were proud to accept the invitation and the chance to exhibit their skills. At the conclusion of the contest, Emperor Antonius Pius was so impressed by their performance that he ordered a statue of Parsman to be built. So began Georgia's international reputation as a center of expert horsemanship.[4]

Horsemanship was a mandatory spectacle during church holidays and other public rituals. More than 360 horse games were known in Georgia. Italian missionary and artist Cristoforo De Castelli, who in 1631 arrived in Georgia with a group of missionaries and remained there until 1654, mentioned: "Having arrived in Kutais [a town in western Georgia], where resides the king of Georgians, they took me to see a game of ball, played by players mounted on horseback. This game is very popular, being played not only by the nobles, but by the king him-

1. Georgia

self."[5] The game's name is "Tskhen-burti" or horse-ball. One of the most exciting horse games in Georgia certainly remains Isindi. It simulates a military battle with spears. Isindi reproduces a battle between groups of riders, using throwing spears 1.5 meters in length, with blunt ends, which have protective heads of leather or rubber. Also very fascinating is the mounted archery game Kabakhi, when a rider at full gallop has to hit the target (a bowl, cup, or any other small object) located on a high pole.

As time passed, the equestrian skills first demonstrated by King Parsman and his cavalry grew in scope and richness. In 1857, fascinated by the techniques of the Georgian horsemen, Russian Czar Alexander II declared an order, mandating that his private convoy would be made up of men from the Caucasus region, especially Georgia. It would

Standing, left to right: Joseph Imnadze, Luka Chkhartishvili, Data Kadjaia, Ushangi Kvitaishvili, Miron Chkonia, Alexander Khukhunaishvili, Pavle Makharadze. *Sitting, middle:* Karaman Imnadze, Ivane Jorbenadze, Irakli Tsintsadze, Nikoloz Antadze. *Sitting, front:* Porphile Kantaria, Konstantine Chkhartishvili, Teophane Kavtaradze, Ivane Baramidze, Simon Oragvelidze, circa 1899.

be called "the private convoy—the private guard of the Caucasian Escadron." The first twenty members of this guard were young men from Tbilisi and Kutaisi, no more than 25 years of age.

From the beginning of the 20th century, the Georgian officers from the Czar's army successfully participated in various competitions held in Russia and Europe. In 1912, Count Chavchavadze took part in the Olympic Games held in Stockholm, Sweden. The same year, for the first time in the history of the Russian Empire, Konstantine Avalishvili won the Liverpool Grand Prize in the steeplechase competition, one of the most complicated horse racing events ever.

In the twenties of the 20th century, many Georgian emigrants started out their activities on new American soil as horsemen. That's how well-known sculptor and author George Papashvily (1898–1978)

Standing, left to right: **Mikha Darsalia, Nikoloz Surguladze, Kirile Khoperia, Mikheil Chkhartishvili, Silovan Kartvelishvili, Ioram Mshvidobadze.** *Sitting, middle:* **unknown, Mr. Cohen and daughter, Dimitri Tsintsadze, Luka Chkhartishvili, Parnaoz Shakarishvili.** *Sitting, front:* **Sergi Gvarjaladze, Solomon Imnadze, Ese Tsintsadze, Kirile Pirtskhalaishvili, United States, 1903.**

describes his first steps in the United States in his book *Anything Can Happen* (1945):

> In Hollywood there wasn't much choice of jobs at that time except to be in the movies. So I went in the casting office, and the next thing I'm in the movies! But they always called me to play a Cossack. No variety.
>
> One day, I forget if I was turning back the hordes of Genghis Khan that time or was I being mean to the Volga boatmen again? Well, anyway, I got disgusted. I said to myself: If I wanted to ride a horse all day and wear a cherkesska [traditional Caucasian male dress] and a fur hat, you could have stayed home in Kobiankari. No, you came in America for something different.[6]

Another Georgian émigré, Prince Dimitri Jorjadze (1898–1985), a nobleman, car racer and playboy, who was exiled after Soviet Russia occupied Georgia in 1921, bought a historic plantation in South Carolina known as Boone Hall. Jorjadze was known as an equestrian genius and top bloodstock-breeder. Most notable of his horses was the world's champion Princequillo, who in 1943 was the fastest distance runner in the United States and who became a two-time leading sire in North America and a seven-time leading broodmare sire in North America.

In particular, the Gurian-Georgians, who live on the mountainous Black Sea Coast, became famous as expert riders and horsemen. From generation to generation, their riding skills improved, becoming more sophisticated and refined.

2. Guria: The Heart of Georgia

Compared to the other parts of the country, Guria is relatively young. It is first mentioned in the annals of the 8th century AD, when in 736 Georgia was invaded by the ferocious Arab leader Murvan ibn Muhamad. He plundered the eastern and western parts of the country and camped out in Guria before a decisive battle. Because he paid no attention to the pleas and groans of the people, he was called Murvan the Deaf. In Guria, heartless people are called Murvanas to this day.

As for the etymology of the name of Guria, some sources claimed that the explanation is based on the following legend. "King Shedat of India decided to build a paradise on earth, thinking that the nation would worship him as a God. But the nobility said that the heavenly garden lacked angels. The king ordered them to bring 'Gurias' (beautiful people) from all over the world to India. But the lord punished the King for his heresy. The story of the king's death reached the gurias in the Caucasus and they decided to settle there. And their land was called Guria."[1]

According to the latter explanation, in the times of Georgia's prosperity (XII–XIII c.), when its borders stretched from Black Sea to Caspian Sea, Guria was situated in the heart of the Georgian territory. The linguistic evidence for above hypothesis is the Mingrelian for "heart"—"Guri." (The Mingrelians are an ethnic subgroup of Georgians.)

Gurian people were well known around Georgia for their courage and audacity. "Gurians are very proud: the sense of self-dignity is very much present in Guria. Aristocracy—"the elite"—is a major feature of Gurian culture. In this regard there is almost no difference between princes and peasants. Each Gurian is fond of showing himself off." This is the way that prominent Georgian-German writer Grigol Robakidze (1881-1962) characterized the Gurians. According to the famous Georgian writer and scholar Jacob Gogebashvili (1840-1912): "A Gurian is

2. Guria

Gurian militants, circa 1879.

talkative, moves fast, is straightforward, and hates hypocrisy. He's explosive, like gunpowder, but calms down easily. Gurians are known for their bravery and swiftness, and they like to learn things." Bordered with an aggressive Muslim world, Georgian-Gurians always had to be prepared to fight the enemy. Carrying arms was common. Once, in the middle of the 19th century, a Gurian nobleman, Bezhan Bolkvadze, came across eight armed Turks in the woods. Bolkvadze didn't get lost: He attacked the Turks, who obviously did not expect such an action. Before the enemy could realize what was happening, Bolkvadze killed two of them and injured two. Four other Turks escaped.[2]

As for Gurian songs, they are just as hot-tempered, quick, and mysterious as the Gurian character itself. When great composer Igor Stravinsky first heard the Gurian song Krimanchuli, he became amazed by the singular vocal technique and exclaimed: "Never in my life have I listened to anything better than this."[3] Lady Colin Campbell, journalist, playwright, editor, and author of a selection of essays, *A Woman's Walks*, describes Georgian "Cossack" songs and their horsemanship:

> The musical song of the Cossacks closes Mr. Baker's exhibition, and the curious minor chanter, with its plaintive inflections, calls up visions of the snow-plains and the retreat from Russia, when the forefathers, no doubt, of these

Gurians in Batumi, circa 1899.

horsemen in scarlet and sheepskins caused so many of the French invaders to leave their bones behind in the land which fire and snow had made invulnerable. They gave an exhibition of horsemanship which reminds one of Dickens' description of the acrobatic boy at Mrs. Leo Hunter's party, who did everything with a chair except sit on it.[4]

Although in the second half of the 19th century Guria was the poorest place in the country, Gurians have always had a thirst for education: "The Gurians are the bravest and most warlike, most chivalrous, most handsome, most hospitable, most educated, although not the most unpractical of the Georgians. Every village has its own library, and even those furthest from the Government post stations provide their own mail service so as to receive the daily papers from Tiflis [Tbilisi], Batum, and Russia."[5] This is a quote from the *Fire and Sword in the Caucasus* by the Italian author, diplomat, and traveler Luigi Villari (1876—1959).

3. From East to West

1887 is believed to be the first year that Georgian-Gurian riders went abroad, although this date has not been verified in either Georgian, British, or American archives. However, a daily newspaper, *The Times* in Philadelphia (July 29, 1888), ran a story about the Russian Czar and the Cossacks, headlined "Cossack and Cowboy," in which Buffalo Bill Cody commented on the riding skills of the Cossacks. "I don't know anything about Cossack riding, because I never saw any of it, but I will guarantee that our men can do anything that Cossacks do and more, too ... I only wish the Russian Government could send us a horse that the cowboys can't ride. That, of course, would be impossible, but if it could be, the horse would be worth his weight in gold."[1] This article appears to prove that Cossacks had never been in America before 1893.

Of all the tales told about the riders, the one most often repeated is the story of their recruitment. The following is a firsthand account, told by the riders to the Academician Amiran Tsamtsishvili. Thomas Oliver (1867–1943), a commissioner, approximately in the winter of 1891 arrived in Western Georgia, Adjara's[2] seaport town Batumi, to locate riders for Buffalo Bill Cody's Wild West in the United States.

In 1889, a Paiute Indian named Wovoka, known as Jack Wilson, who worked on a ranch, became ill with a fever. He believed had been taken to heaven in a vision that the Great Spirit was coming back to the world to drive the white man out for the return of the old-time life and superiority of the Indians. Wovoka, a new messiah, preached a doctrine of peace and faithfulness. If the Indians refrained from violence, and if they performed the Ghost Dance, they could hasten the resurrection of dead relatives and the restoration of days of Indian prosperity. The first Oklahoma Territory Ghost Dance was held in Watonga in April 1890. In September 1890, about three thousand Indians of different tribes gathered on the South Canadian River and danced every night for two weeks. The Ghost Dance was a peaceful movement, but the news that Sitting Bull, Great Sioux warrior and former performer of Buffalo Bill's Wild

3. From East to West

Georgian horsemen.

West, was Ghost Dancing caused the government to panic. One Indian agent wrote to officials: "Indians are dancing in the snow and are wild and crazy.... We need protection and we need it now."[3] The government thought that anything that would unite American Indians would be dangerous, even if it preached peace. And with Sitting Bull involved, it might turn into an uprising.

Buffalo Bill Cody was asked by General Nelson Miles to determine the Wild West ex-performer Sitting Bull's role in the movement. Cody packed gifts for the chief, but the local Indian agent prevented him from meeting with Sitting Bull. Certainly not a central figure in the Ghost Dance, Sitting Bull was killed just days before the massacre at Wounded Knee, when Indian police were sent to arrest him. Soon, on December 29, 1890, the military surrounded the camp of the Sioux Indians and tried to disarm them. When the Indians refused, commanding officers ordered soldiers to search teepees and the Indians for weapons. There was a quarrel, and a young man named Black Coyote, insulted by the rough treatment, fired a shot that developed into a gunfight. An officer was shot, and the soldiers retaliated with a deadly volley at close range. Some Indians managed to shoot back, while from a low hill four Hotchkiss guns began to spew explosive shells into the scattering Sioux. It cost the lives of at least 150 men, women, and children, as well as that of Chief Big Foot. Twenty-five soldiers were also killed, most of them by stray bullets of associates.[4] On both sides there were many wounded. The massacre at Wounded Knee was the final conflict in the American Indian Wars and the almost 300 hundred years of resistance to the American government.

Buffalo Bill's Wild West portrayed Native Americans as warlike, aggressive savages. In such scenes as "The Battle of Summit Springs," "Attack on a Settler's Cabin," and "Famous Attack on the Deadwood Stage Coach," Indians often were portrayed attacking innocent villagers, raping the wives of white settlers, or scalping unfortunate cavalrymen, and white men and women were rescued by Buffalo Bill and his men. This certainly made for exciting entertainment, but was quite inaccurate historically. But behind the show curtains, Buffalo Bill proved his loyalty to the Native Americans on his Wild West tours. They were given the same freedoms of any other performers. "We have very little trouble with any of the natives," Cody reported. "They are a quiet, peaceable crowd, and our general policy is to let them settle any little difference that may arise among themselves; indeed, we rarely ever have occasion to interfere." "Cody's treatment of the Native Americans earned him special status among governmental agencies. Though there were many other western shows, none except Buffalo Bill's Wild West were allowed to hire directly from the reservations. Cody alone was trusted in this regard."[5]

It must be noted that after the Wounded Knee massacre, the nineteen leaders of the Ghost Dance were imprisoned in Fort Sheridan in Illinois. There they posed a problem for the army, which was under pressure to release them but didn't want to return them to the reservation, fearing they would revive the Ghost Dance. Buffalo Bill found the solution: the prisoners would come with the Wild West to Europe. All but four of the leaders joined the Wild West with their families and friends.[6]

Under the influence of Wild West shows, Western movies used to depict Indians as savages, as forces of nature that stood in the way of civilization. John Ford often has been criticized for his portrayal of Native Americans. But in the *Cheyenne Autumn*, he showed how badly

Native Americans had been treated by the government and made an attempt to apologize to the Indians for his portrayal of them in some of his earlier films. "I had wanted to make it for a long time. I've killed more Indians than Custer, Beecher, and Chivington put together, and people in Europe always want to know about the Indians. There are two sides to every story, but I wanted to show their point of view for a change. Let's face it, we've treated them very badly—it's a blot on our shield; we've cheated and robbed, killed, murdered, massacred, and everything else, but they kill one white man and, God, out come the troops."[7]

In the above-mentioned *Buffalo Bill*, director William Wellman shows Buffalo Bill Cody as a real American hero, spending much time in vigorous protest against the harsh treatment accorded the Native Americans in his earlier days as an Indian fighter—a rather unusual take for a mid–1940s western. Only from the 1960s, in revisionist Westerns, did Hollywood begin to revise American heroes and icons and to portray native people realistically. Unlike Wellman's film, Robert Altman, in *Buffalo Bill and The Indians, or Sitting Bull's History Lesson* (1976) shows Buffalo Bill as a hollow fraud. It was released in America's bicentennial year and commented on American history, the politics of show business, and the exploitation of Native Americans by greedy entrepreneurs.[8]

After the Wounded Knee massacre, Buffalo Bill didn't learn he would be allowed to hire Native Americans again until March of 1891. While Cody had been in Dakota, Nate Salsbury, Cody's business partner and Wild West's general manager, who had stayed in Europe, focused his creative energies on coming up a way to replace the Indians if that became necessary. He was prepared to carry through his original plan for an exhibition of horsemanship, in which riders from many parts of the world would be contrasted with the American cowboys, Indians, and vaqueros. In distant South Africa, South America, Arabia, and Russia, emissaries were set to work.[9] This is confirmed by the 1893 Official Program for Buffalo Bill's Wild West and Congress of Rough Riders of the World, which stated: "In pursuance of their intention to assemble together, at the World's Fair, a congress of the representative horsemen of the world, Messrs. Cody and Salsbury have had their agents in all parts of the earth, looking for rough riders who could compete with or excel the original riders of the Wild West, the native product of America."[10]

In Batumi, Thomas Oliver stopped at the home of James C. Chambers, the American Consul, who had held his post since 1890. (The Batumi consulate had been opened in 1886.) "Chambers was only a part-time consul; his salary was paid by the Standard Oil Company, owned by John D. Rock-

Kirile Jorbenadze.

efeller. Rockefeller had sent Chambers to Batumi to gather intelligence on Standard Oil's competitor, the Nobel Company, which had opened the rail line from Baku to Batumi to ship Caspian oil to Black Sea tankers."[11]

An employee of Chambers, a fellow named Kirile Jorbenadze, who was on familiar terms with some of the riders in Guria, offered help to find brilliant Georgian horsemen. Jorbenadze was a woodcutter before he became an assistant for James Chambers. Kirile kept a close relationship over the years with Chambers, who would send his son to Batumi to stay with Kirile during holidays. Kirile ran his own restaurant, named Florida, and became a shareholder in the hotel London in Batumi. But when Bolsheviks came, they confiscated all his property. Oliver accepted, and soon the two men, plus vice-consul Harry Briggs, departed to the village of Lanchkhuti. On the way there they stopped at village of Bakhvi, where they visited Ivane Makharadze—nicknamed "Matrakha" ("Matrakha" in Georgian: "the man who carried the whip")— a distinguished rider who promised Oliver that he would be responsible for signing up other riders.

Bakhvi is a few kilometers from the town of Ozurgeti. Ozurgeti is a regional administrative center of Guria. It is a big, picturesque village, with remaining traditional Gurian odas—two- or three-room wooden houses built on high stone pillars. Bakhvi was known for famous Georgians who were born there: artists Dimitri Shevardnadze and Shalva Kikodze, the Bishop of Imereti[12] Gabriel Kikodze, playwright Nino Nakahshidze, and opera singer David Andguladze. It was a center of revolutionary movement in Guria in 1905 and known for the so-called Bakhvi manifest, when peasants made demands to Russian government, which included: the return to their homes of persons exiled to Siberia without trial; the withdrawal of troops recently sent to intimidate the population; abolition of censorship and establishment of freedom of the press and publication, etc. It did not work and was bloodily ended.

Iveria weekly confirms the story of Thomas Oliver's arrival in an article published in June (#124), 1892, "A visiting dignitary from England has arrived in Batumi and stayed at the councils. A fellow dressed in long, typical Georgian dress, working for a consul, caught the guest's attention. He asked the fellow to help him collect twelve good-looking, similarly outfitted fine riders. He also mentioned that he would pay good money and bring them back in six months' time at his own expenses."

Thomas Oliver was a remarkable character. He was born on May 9, 1867, in Toronto, Canada, in a family of circus performers. He spent his childhood on the road with his parents. His parents came to London when he was five years old and joined the Manly circus, which was starting for the Caucasus. Perhaps that's how he ended up spending some time in Tbilisi. However, another version of the story relates that at the age of three he was kidnapped and taken to Russia, where a French family adopted him. Later, he came to the Caucasus and settled in Tbilisi. During the following years, Oliver traveled across the Russian Empire with various circuses and became familiar with the Georgians' riding skills. This implies that he didn't come to Georgia "blindfolded." Later, he interpreted for the Georgian riders from 1892 to 1896, presumably in Russian, or, quite possibly, in Georgian. Riders called him Tommy; his nickname was "Cossack" Tom.

> Not being able to speak English, the visitors have brought an interpreter with them, who spoke English, French, Russian, and Tartar. A romantic, though pathetic, interest attaches to this man. He is a native of Manchester, and his name is Thomas Oliver. His parents came to London when he was five years old, and joined the Manly circus, which was starting for the Caucasus. By some accident he got left behind at Tbilisi, and has since earned his living amongst the various circuses traveling in that part of the world, Russians being extremely fond of that kind of entertainment. He now returns to his native land after an absence of eighteen years. He is trying to find his parents, but knows nothing about them beyond the fact that his Mother's name was Mary Lizzie and that he had a sister.[13]

Oliver worked with Buffalo Bill and the "Cossacks" until 1896. His obituary states: "Thomas Oliver, seventy-six, retired circus and vaudeville acrobat, died in Defiance, Ohio, September 5, 1943. He spent his entire life in show business. He was a contortionist and acrobat and traveled with circuses, including Ringling Bros., vaudeville and at one time had his own show, the Oliver Family Shows. Surviving were three daughters, a son, four grandchildren, and a sister."[14]

The following story may also help explain why the riders from Guria and not from other regions of Georgia or the Caucasus were selected to perform in Wild West shows. Ivane Makharadze, the Georgian riders' first acclaimed leader, spent his childhood in native Bakhvi. He had three brothers, Silibistro, Pavle, and Alexandre.

The story goes that when he was fourteen years old, his father asked

3. From East to West

Ivane Makharadze.

him to ride to a distant village—Bakhmaro. Fond of horse riding, the young Ivane was more than happy to oblige. He fast rode till he got thirsty and dismounted at the spring. The sweaty horse, left unattended, gulped down too much cold water and died. Ivane came back with only a saddle on his back and accepted a deserved thrashing from his father.

The boy, ashamed of his failure, could not tolerate his offense and ran away to Batumi.

Batumi is one of the oldest cities in Georgia. Its initial form—Batus—must have derived from the Greek word meaning "deep." In antique times the local population used to have active trade relations with the neighboring as well as distant countries.

Batumi has always been distinguished by a favorable natural and strategic location. From the 18th century, Batumi was under Ottoman rule. After the Turkish-Russian war of 1877–1878 and Berlin Treaty, Batumi became an inseparable constituent part of Georgia. In 1878–1886, Batumi Port was announced as "Porto Franco," which fostered the further development of the city. After the construction of the Baku-Batumi railway system (1883), reconstruction of the Batumi port, and connection to Baku via pipelines (1897–1907), Batumi became an important sea terminal along the Black Sea littoral. Caspian Sea oil products were transferred from this location to other countries. In 1888, Batumi was officially granted city status, and the first mayor of Batumi was elected. Moreover, Batumi became the main Russian oil port on the Black Sea. The city was placed under the direct control of the General Government of Georgia only in 1903. In 1918 and 1920, the city was governed by the Ottomans and the British respectively. After becoming a Soviet State, in 1921, Adjara, with its center in Batumi, was declared an autonomous republic. It retains this status to the present day.

In Batumi, Ivane bumped into two young men from another Georgian region, Racha,[15] who were employed on one of the ships. With their help, Ivane was introduced to the ship's captain. The captain grew fond of the short but lively fellow and gave him a job. The ship weighed anchor the next day and arrived in New York harbor almost a month later. By that time, fed up with his exhausting and boring job, Ivane quit and, after days of aimless wandering, picked up another job at a bakery. Ivane worked hard for the baker, since he had no other way to make a living. He had to work to earn enough to live and learn English. Once he learned enough English, he ran away. The rest of the story is a bit vague, but a year or so later he surfaced as a cleaner at one of the circuses in New York. His diligence and penchant for horses caught the attention of an Arab rider employed by the circus, and he was again hired. From this point forward, Ivane was responsible for taking care of the horses.

He worked really hard. With his circus earnings, Ivane bought his first horse and soon was asked to perform trick riding for the circus. Clad in his national dress, he pioneered the trick of grabbing coins while riding. His successful debut allowed him to buy a second horse and become increasingly independent. Only now, when he had enough personal savings, did Ivane dare to send a message to his parents telling them where he was. In 1885, shortly before Thomas Oliver's appearance in Georgia, Ivane Makharadze returned to his homeland. This story suggests that Oliver might have known about Makharadze's odyssey in America, and as a result, he knew perfectly well where to look for the Georgian

Alexander Tskvitishvili.

riders. It must be noted that the tale of Ivane's travel to America is not documented. In an interview with the *Star* (May 31, 1892), Makharadze said that "they never before been out of their own country," which confirms that it was his first trip outside Georgia.

In a little while, the group of ten riders, mostly from the Gurian villages, Chibati and Lanchkhuti, underwent training and sewed six pairs in different colors of the national dress, the chokha. Their chokhas were orange, yellow, green, motley purple—colors that Georgian men occasionally used in their dress. Apparently it was the part of the spectacle, to catch audience attention: "The dress of the riders is picturesque in the extreme and composed of such colors as civilized races know nothing of—untempered browns and yellows and crimson, the product of primitive dyes."[16] William E. Curtis had a contrary opinion about Georgian national dress: "We are accustomed to see the Cossacks at Buffalo Bill's great moral show in dark gray coats, but the Georgians, whose costume is precisely similar in every particular, affect bright colors—reds and blue of various shades, grays and browns, as well as whites and blacks, according to their taste, and some of them have their shakos of Persian lamb dyed the same shade as their coats."

One newspaper described the "Cossack" dress: "The Cossacks are dressed in peculiar yellow coats, wrapped at the waist, and small circular caps of the same material. On both breasts of the coat are two receptacles, as if for cartridges, but which are merely ornamental."[17] (The decorative cartridge pocket is for holding flint rifle or pistol cartridges. The pockets were lined with tubes made of wood or bone.) Usually, to differ from other members of the group, the chief "Cossack" wore white chokha: "The Cossacks were lying flat of their backs, stroking their beards, singing softly, perhaps of a sweetheart in far-away Russia. One or two were smoking, puffing ring after ring of light blue smoke from their thin lips. Their commander is a Prince, and is called Prince Luca. He is the one who wears the white coat."[18]

Soon they departed to Batumi. Each "Cossack" was armed with dagger, saber, pistol, and rifle. "The arms of the Cossack soldiers are quite rich in ornament; all of their daggers, swords, and old-fashioned horse pistols, being embellished with chasing of gold and silver. The men, besides being centaur-like riders, are expert swordsmen as well, and affect razor-edged sabers with which they can snuff a candle while going at a full gallop or dissect an enemy's head at the axial vertebra with equal facility."[19] On one occasion Luka Chkhartishvili showed his pistol to a reporter: "eighteen inches long, weight two and a half pounds … made of solid silver, with a butt of some rare wood" and claimed that pistol had belonged to his grandfather and was a century old.[20]

In Batumi, the ticketing agent gave them their second-class tickets, valued at 175 francs ($35),[21] and accompanied the ten Georgians to gather their passports. Each in turn stood before the administrative clerk, presented his papers, and furnished his name, age, and village. The clerk recorded the passport information in Georgian, Russian, and French. Wild West female "Cossack" Frida Mgaloblishvili explained to one newspaper correspondent: "The Cossacks … had only come to America for the sake of seeing the country. They travel on passports from their government that have to be carefully visaed by all the consuls through whose stations they pass, in order that they may return to their fatherland with an official record of all their proceedings since leaving there."²² Every rider after paying 15 rubles (the price varied from 15 to 20 rubles) received his passport. Usually the passports were signed by the military governor of Kutaisi (district of western Georgia) or his assistant, and then they were given permission to travel to Europe and America because of family circumstances.

William F. Cody in one interview described his difficulties in obtaining Russian Cossacks for his exhibition:

> Hardest of all to secure are the Cossacks. Pulling an elephant's tooth is simple work compared to the diplomatic dentistry necessary in pulling a Cossack out of the jaw of Russia. Nine years ago I got my first batch of Cossacks through the aid of General John C. New of Indianapolis, then United States consul at London. He succeeded in unwinding the miles of red tape in which the process was swathed. With the exception of Prince Luka—prince in this instance meaning one of thousands of hetman, or chief of band—all the Cossacks are new each year. Even Luka, caught in the meshes of the red tape, was one season unable to join us. He slapped a Russian's face or something like that, and the slapped gentleman prevented Luka from getting his passport. And unless you have a passport out of Russia, you can't get in again. When the show was over last year, Luka as usual took his Cossacks back to Batumi, distant several days from Odessa, and in the spring brought a new lot of the Czar's Rough Riders to Odessa, where our agent inspected and selected this season's contingent.²³

Group leaders were mostly referred to in the lists as "Prince." In fact, only some of the riders were of noble origin. The rest were mostly peasants from around the Ozurgeti and Lanchkhuti. Apparently, it was a publicity stunt to attract more people.

Soon they boarded a steamship sailing between Batumi and Marseilles, with a stop in Constantinople for passenger pickup. After two days, they arrived at the Bosporus Strait. New passengers entered the ship, and it continued across the Marmara Sea into the Aegean and Mediterranean Seas. Sailing nine more days brought them to Marseilles, France. The Georgians passed through customs and boarded a special train headed to Paris. They visited the offices of C.M. Ercole and soon found themselves on the French coast aboard a packet steamer bound for England. The so-called "Russian Cossacks," with their chief, Prince Ivane Makharadze, arrived at Earl's Court on May 26.²⁴

4. Down in Albion: The Russians Are Coming!

"The Tower, the Parliament, and Westminster are older institutions in London than Buffalo Bill's show, but when the New Zealander sits on the London Bridge and looks over his ancient manuscript of Murray's Guide-book, he is going to turn first to the Wild West. At present everyone know where it is, from the gentleman on Piccadilly to the dirtiest coster in the remotest slum of Whitechapel. The cabman may have to scratch his head to recall places where the traveler desires to go, but when the "Wild West" is asked for, he gathers his reins and uncoils his whip without ceremony. One should no longer ride the deserts of Texas or the rugged uplands of Wyoming to see the Indians and the pioneers, but should go to London. It is also quite unnecessary to brave fleas and the police of the Czar to see Cossacks, or to tempt the waves which roll between New York and the far-off Argentine to study the 'gauchos.' It is all in London. The Cossacks and 'gauchos' are the latest addition, and they nearly complete the array of wild riders." This is a description of 1892 Wild West London by famed artist Frederic Remington.[1]

The British newspaper *The Weekly Dispatch* reported its first account of the Cossack riders on May 8, 1892. That was the riders' first documented trip abroad, to England. A similar, but shorter account of that trip appeared in the Georgian newspaper *Iveria*. It recorded briefly, "Batumi: Here's the list of Georgians taken to London by a French agent: Ivane Makharadze, Dimitri Mgaloblishvili, Vaso Ckhonia, Levanti Jorbenadze, Luka Chkhartishvili, Mose Gigineishvili, Irakli Ckhonia, Besarion Tsintsadze, and Meliton Tsintsadze." In an interview granted to *The Oracle* (May 28, 1892), Nate Salsbury, the Buffalo Bill's Wild West show's general manager, confirmed it:

"I understand you have got a troupe of Cossacks in Camp, Mr. Salsbury?

"Yes, they arrived last night. They come from beyond Tiflis, near the extreme of the Caucasus Mountains. They are headed by Prince Ivane Makharadze, and are under the charge of an interpreter called Tom, whose

4. Down in Albion

Standing, left to right: **Besarion Tsintsadze, Mose Gigineishvili, Vaso Chkonia, Data Chkonia, Meliton Tsintsadze. Sitting, left to right: Luka Chkhartishvili, Levanti Jorbenadze, Irakli Chkonia, Dimitri Mgaloblishvili. Reclining, left to right: interpreter Thomas Oliver, unknown, Ivane Makharadze, London, 1892.**

life is a romance in itself. He [Tom] was of English parentage and was born in London. He was kidnapped when less than three years of age and taken to Russia. He was adopted by a French family, and has lived in the Caucasus ever since. These are genuine Don Cossacks, and we claim they are the first of their class who have ever left their country except in a war. The Cossack is different from a cowboy inasmuch as he is really a soldier and a part of the Russian Army. Their riding consists mainly of tricks on horseback, and I am very anxious to see what they can do in that line. We cannot try them yet, as their wiry little horses need rest after their long journey. These men were brought over by the energy and enterprise of M. Ercolè, the great Parisian agent, who was nearly in prison half a dozen times over his job. We have had to guarantee the return of these men to the Russian government, our Ambassador in St. Petersburg being the guarantor. We shall probably get these men to ride next week."

"As Mr. Salsbury spoke, several Cossacks approached. They were apparently sauntering around the camp out of curiosity, and presented a picturesque appearance with their astrakhan caps and long dark red coats and top boots. They are small, undersized, but wiry-looking men."[2]

It was also said that Prince Makharadze might have travelled with an entourage suit and demanded the social reception befitting his rank, but that he preferred to be a humble worker with the rest of the company.[3] Their American employers wanted to sell tickets, of course, and the best way to do that was to make these Russians popular heroes. As we can see, the riders, abiding by the orders from show's owners, would perform their respective roles like high-class actors, although often they were tempted to tell the truth. We will talk more about it below.

One reporter asked Ivane Makharadze how he liked London. "We like it," he replied. "The railway running under the earth is strange, and the town is large. Ordinary railways we know. There is one at home, at Batumi, which we have seen when we came from our village. But to like this country as well as our own, that would be impossible. How could we? We came because we get more money here than we can earn at home, but we have only come for six months. Then we go back to our wives and children."

Then he was asked why they had not brought their families. "Why have you not brought them? The Cossack women are good-looking and their dress is beautiful, and your little ones would be as happy in this garden during the summer as they are at home."

"No, our women would not come. Not for anything. They have remained behind to look after the grapes, the maize, the horses, the old people, and the children, while we are away."[4]

By that time, the British were well aware of Buffalo Bill's traveling extravaganza. The show had been introduced to the English public at Queen Victoria's golden jubilee in 1887. It was a smash, despite having no so-called "Cossacks." Queen Victoria attended a Wild West performance and stood when the American flag was presented. Buffalo Bill remembered:

> Her Majesty rose from her seat and bowed deeply and impressively towards the banner. The whole court party rose, the ladies bowed, the generals present saluted, and the English noblemen took off their hats.... For the first time in history, since the Declaration of Independence, a sovereign of Great Britain has saluted a star-spangled banner, and that banner was carried by a member of Buffalo Bill's Wild West![5]

"Russian Cossacks first joined Buffalo Bill's Wild West in London in 1892," wrote Sarah J. Blackstone in her book *Buckskins, Bullets, and*

Business: The History of Wild West Show. "The original group numbered ten and ranged in age from 18 to 25. Their leader or commander was Prince Ivan Makharadze. They were contacted in Russia by Cody's agent C. M. Ercole, who made all the necessary arrangements for bringing them to London, and they were advertised as the first group of Cossacks ever to leave Russia." According to the *Daily Telegraph* (June 4, 1892), Ivan Makharadze and his band weren't the first "Cossacks" to have visited London. In 1814, Napoleonic wars participant Count Platoff with troupe of (real) Don Cossacks stayed in London for some time. It turned out Platoff had an overwhelming fondness for vodka and was a passionate admirer of champagne. The newspaper also admits that he had a rooted dislike of soap and water.

Earlier, another British newspaper, *Pictorial World* (May 28, 1892), wrote, "A new feature is to be added to the already sufficiently attractive show at Earl's Court [which held the London International Horticultural Exhibition, where Wild West would be the centerpiece]. On Monday

Kirile Pirtskhalaishvili with wife.

last there arrived some Don Cossacks, and these, we understand are to take part in the performance. Many persons will be attracted to the show if only to see these warriors."

The first group of riders caused great excitement in London because it was the first time, since 1814, that Londoners had encountered the so-called "Cossacks." According to *The Illustrated London News* (June 18, 1892), "Buffalo Bill's Wild West from the North American prairies may be seen here again, positively for the last time in Europe, and the Cossacks of the Russian Caucasus, famous military horsemen, under command of their Hetman, Prince Ivan Makharadze, perform equal feats of equestrian prowess." The Georgians' daggers and swords, and especially their eye-catching national outfits decorated with pockets for cartridges, were a special topic of conversation, and aficionados took them for miniature sticks of dynamite. "Each [Cossack] was armed with a great dagger, a thirty-two inch muzzle-loading pistol and long Caucasian rifle, and carried his powder in rows of little tubes hung across the chest."[6]

In another quote from *Iveria*:

> There is a band of Georgian horsemen in London who are currently amusing the gloomy sons of that foggy town with their riding skills, dancing and songs. Reportedly, the British, who assumed they were Russians, honor them with special treatment and the local newspapers praise their strong physique, dances and sad songs. Some Georgian riders are in London, and they amused the frowning and reserved people of England with their show and songs. It's interesting who these Georgians are. Since your newspaper has its eye on Georgians all over the world, I considered it necessary to inform you about the Georgians who left for London six months ago. They are from Guria, namely from Chibati and Lanchkhuti. They belong to different levels of society, but some of them are aznauri [noblemen in Georgian]. You might be surprised imagining Gurians in London. But there is nothing surprising: two months ago the Consul of England in Batumi hosted a rich man from abroad. This person was called an English Lord in Georgia. The guest was fascinated by the appearance and cloths of the Gurians, who were present at the meeting. He asked his Gurian host to find 12 handsome fellows, good riders and singers, in order to take them to England. The promise was to pay 50 rubles each, per month, and cover all travel expenses to and from England. They obtained the permission from the Governor, and two months ago they left for abroad.

Reporters followed the Georgians everywhere; they wanted to know everything about them.

4. Down in Albion

> The long lazy morning is over; the fun begins. There is some movement in the background of the white tents opposite to the camp of the Redskins, where the ten Cossacks are quartered at the Horticultural Exhibition, and one by one the giants arise from their beds, where they have been smoking the inevitable cigarette. So much of Russian civilization has trickled even into the Caucasian district behind Batoum, where, until a few weeks ago, they have lived among the vineyards and maize-fields that they all have taken to the papyrus—the tiny cigarette without which between his lips the true Russian gentleman does not consider himself fully dressed. The ends of the papyrus are thrown away, and the ten prepare for action.[7]

A few day of busy rehearsals, and the "Cossacks" were ready for performance. The party of mounted figures to burst upon the arena from behind the painted scenery were "Cossacks" riding on ponies. "Cossacks" were headed by the Prince. Newspapers described the Georgians' arresting appearance in the arena. "The performance began with what perhaps had best be termed a musical ride, the horsemen cantering slowly round the ring while they sang a strange, weird refrain, which was at once harmonious and barbaric. The strain they lifted was touched with a Chopinesque melancholy, and to the imaginative ear clearly suggested the sadness of the illimitable snow-covered steppe"[8] Their riding technique was described in many articles:

> A band of Cossacks from the Caucasus have come to town. They were brought here by Colonel Cody and are now one of the most brilliant features of the Wild West Show at Earl's Court.... It is difficult to imagine more difficult feats of horsemanship than those performed by the cowboys on the bucking bronchos. Antonio Escoval, the leader of the Mexicans, handles a horse as though he were a direct descendant of the centaurs. The Indians sit a bare-backed steed as if they had grown there, yet all of them have something to learn from Prince Ivan Makharadze's Cossacks.[9]

Georgians made an indelible impression on the public. It is well demonstrated in the "Dreams of Susan Spragg" that was published in *The London Serio-Comic Journal* (July 15, 1892). She described it in the letter to her friend, after seeing the Cossacks at Earle's court. Susan dreamed that when she, with her boyfriend, visited Wild West show, one fierce-looking Cossack beat up her boyfriend and took Susan to a faraway land of Tartary.[10] But there, the handsome Mazeppa king released her, and they fell in love with each other.

When the so-called Cossacks arrived, the time had come to adopt

Gurians on parade, 1900.

the subtitle "Congress of Rough Riders of the World," which was first used when the show returned to London in the spring of 1892.[11]

> "While we were in England," said John Burke, Wild West's press agent, "the criticism was continually being made that there were Cossacks or South [American] gauchos who could ride as well as our cowboys. So in 1892 when we returned to England, we decided to get some of these other horsemen. We secured some Cossacks and gauchos. Then we had our Mexicans, and we added some Arabs to the aggregation. Then was coined the phrase "Rough Riders of the world," which has since been used in so many different ways.[12]

According to the famous author, Pulitzer Prize and Oscar winner Larry McMurtry,

> On big ranches, half-broken horses were referred to as the "rough string," and the cowboys whose job it was to improve their behavior might have been called "rough riders."[13]
>
> It is believed that Theodore Roosevelt adopted this name for his regiment in battle for San Juan Hill from Cody, but according to some sources, the future president had used this term six years earlier in a letter to Henry Cabot Lodge: "I think there is some good fighting stuff among these harum-scarum roughriders out there."[14]

5. On Her Majesty's Service

Meanwhile, the news about the "Cossack" horsemanship reached the royal family's ears, and soon the show's manager, Nate Salsbury, received a note from Queen Victoria's Equerry, General Sir Henry Ponsonby, which stated that "Her Majesty will be highly honoured if the Wild West managers could make it convenient to let their Cossack riders come to Windsor and show their wonderful proficiency on horseback to Her Majesty, members of her family and the Royal Household."[1]

Nate Salsbury determined to make a good job of it. He later recalled: "This polite request was constructed, as it always is in England, to be a mild sort of command…. As the Cossacks only consumed about twelve minutes in their performance, I concluded that, no matter how startling it would be, it would hardly compensate for all the trouble of getting them dawn to Windsor, so I determined to take the whole outfit, and do something worthy of the occasion."[2] He hired a train of cars, loaded the outfit, and took it down to Windsor. The troupe, about forty men with their horses, was conveyed at Her Majesty's expense by special Great Western train to Windsor. When Buffalo Bill's Wild West cast arrived at Windsor, they were greeted by a huge crowd, which had gathered about the railway station and lined the streets along which the procession passed. The party was cheered throughout its progress to Windsor Castle.

"On entering the archways, Mr. Cody and Salsbury were received by Major General Sir John C. McNeill, K.C.B., who said that the Queen was anxious to view from her window the entry of the troupe into the arena, so Buffalo Bill at the head of the motley procession of cowboys, Indians, Cossacks, and South American Gauchos paraded under the Queen's windows and, after performing several maneuvers, proceeded to the place selected for the exhibition."[3]

The tennis lawn grounds were enclosed by sheepfold fences for the arena. A canvas and carpeted tent for the Queen and her guests was thrown up.

> The grounds had been enclosed with hurdles trimmed with red bunting, and in the center of the terrace a small pavilion, surmounted by the Royal arms, had been erected. The spaces on either side were crowded with aristocratic personages, a special train having brought a number of the Queen's guests to the castle. Promptly at the hour fixed for the show to commence the Queen came forth from the castle, attended by Princess Beatrice and her children and Princess Christian. She entered a little pony carriage, led by a groom and attended by two gillies and some Indian servants, and the party then proceeded to the pavilion. The Queen was attired in a black dress of the plainest description and wore a queer looking straw bonnet. Arriving near the pavilion the Queen was carefully lifted from her carriage and walked, with the aid of a stick which she carried, to the seat which had been prepared for her in the center of the pavilion. When the royal party had settled in their places, a signal was given and the entertainment was at once begun.[4]

On June 25, 1892, Wild West show members and the "Cossacks," lead by Ivane Makharadze, held a twelve-minute command performance in front of the Queen, the royal family, and other members of the aristocracy.

Here is an extract from Queen Victoria's evening journal:

> We went on to the East Terrace, and watched from a tent, open in front, a sort of Buffalo Bill performance, on the lawn below. It was extremely well arranged, & an excellent representation of what we had also seen five years ago at Earl's Court. There were Cowboys, Red Indians, Mexicans, Argentines taking part, and then a wonderful riding display by Cossacks, accompanied by curious singing, and a war dance by the Indians. There were extraordinary buck jumping horses, shooting at glass balls by Col. Cody, and display of cracking huge long whips. The whole was a very pretty wild sight, which lasted an hour. At the conclusion of the performance, all advanced in line at a gallop & stopped suddenly. Col. Cody was brought up for me to speak to him. He is still a very handsome man, but now got a grey beard.[5]

Before the performance Queen Victoria requested that someone connected with the show should joined the royal party to explain anything she might not understand. Salsbury volunteered.

> After I was introduced to the Queen, I gave the signal to begin, and took my place beside the Queen's place... Noticing that I was standing, and uncovered, Her Majesty said, "Mr. Salsbury, please put on your hat, as I feel a strong draught here, and please take a chair."

5. On Her Majesty's Service

> "Your Majesty," said I, "I'm very comfortable."
>
> "But I would be more comfortable if you would take a chair."
>
> "All this is very commonplace I know, and I would not record it here except that it struck me at the time as being very thoughtful on the part of a woman who is not obliged to consider anything while in the pursuit of pleasure. Being an American, I followed the etiquette of such an occasion by addressing the Queen as Madame, after the first acknowledgment of her imperial title. An Englishman would have been required to address the Queen constantly as Majesty."[6]

During the show, Nate Salsbury sat beside Queen and explained each act.

> Our performance lasted the better part of an hour and a quarter, and during that time the Queen evinced the utmost interest in all she saw, and plied me with questions innumerable regarding the people in the show. And withal, she displayed a nice discrimination in her inquiries, which were all of a sensible, information seeking sort... At a point in the performance when the Cossacks were doing their horseback work, Prince Henry of Battenberg, who was standing in the rear of the pavilion, said to the Queen in German: "Mamma, do you think they are really Cossack?" Before the Queen had time to reply to him, I said [Salsbury was a fluent speaker of several languages], "I beg to assure you, sir, that everything and everybody you see in the entertainment are exactly what we represent it or them to be."
>
> Her Majesty turned to the Prince and said, "Prince, I think we had better speak English for the rest of the afternoon." Princess Beatrice, who was sitting beside the queen, was much amused at her husband's discomfiture, and smilingly said to him, "Mon chere, vous averz recu' votre preiere lecon Americaine." ["My Dear, you have just received your first American lesson."] I immediately replied, "Oh, Madam, J'espere non." ["Oh, Madam, I hope not."] At this there was a general laugh, which I wish Burke could have heard, for he could have used the incident in his own way in his description of the affair.[7]

The "Cossacks" proved by far the most popular of the world rough riders, with their colorful costumes and unorthodox feats of horsemanship, so much so that they became a necessary feature of even the smallest of Wild West shows.[8]

Philip Frank Eliot, Dean of Windsor, described the event in a letter to his mother dated the following day:

> It was really a very pretty sight. The performance took place on the lawn in front of the East Terrace ... and the Queen and all the guests etc. sat on the Terrace itself. Unfortunately it was a dull evening, with no sun. Certainly they performed some wonderful feats of horsemanship. The Queen sug-

gested that her equerries might try to ride the "bucking" horses! But they were not willing.[9]

The entertainment was of the usual character and concluded shortly before six o'clock, when the troupe rode up in front of the Royal Pavilion and finally saluted the Queen.

> When the show was over, the Queen requested that Cody be presented to her, and after thanking me for assisting her to enjoy the Wild West, she arose and was escorted to her carriage by her ever-present body guard of gillies. I sent for Cody, who came in his buckskins, and he was presented to the Queen, just before she started on her afternoon drive around the grounds of the castle. Her Majesty was very gracious to Cody, and complimented him very highly for the delightful afternoon she had enjoyed, and wished him good luck for the future. Cody and I were then invited to the Equerry's apartments, where we were urged to partake of a lunch. We compromised by another act of self-sacrifice on my part, for as Cody did not drink anything that summer, I did duty for both of us in a glass of wine. The whole thing was delightfully informal, and wound up by our each being presented with a memento of the occasion in the Queen's name. Cody received a beautiful watch charm, and I was complimented with a scarf pin, set in diamonds, and bearing the Royal Monogram.[10]

Nate Salsbury does not accidentally mention Cody's drinking. In 1901 he would write: "When he drinks he forgets honor, reputation, friend, and obligation, in his mad eagerness to fill his hide with rotgut of any kind."[11] In his autobiography, Cody states that he started drinking around the age of fourteen. Alcohol figures into many of his exploits and adventures, but he was convinced that drinking never interfered with his work. In his later years, with his health beginning to fail, he quit drinking alcohol.

Whereas the Indians had fascinated Queen Victoria five years before, this time, as author Tom F. Cunningham remarked, the Queen was particularly taken with the "Cossacks" during a second royal command performance.[12] According to some riders, charmed by the spectacle, Her Majesty Queen Victoria presented the Georgians with a gold engraved album with photos of their performance. Presumably, the album was kept at Ivane Makharadze's American-style house in Guria and was destroyed during a fire. Nothing was saved. Rumor says that the fire was not an accident. According to a family member, a pile of wood placed at the only entrance to the house was set on fire. Ivane and his wife Nino hardly escaped. They lost all the memorabilia from Ivane's Wild West riding

5. On Her Majesty's Service

career, including a medal that bore the form of galloping horses, presented by the International Academy of Horseman.[13] British society expressed appreciation by issuing a letter of gratitude signed by 20,000 people.

The Russian newspaper *Moskovskie Vedomosti* wrote the same day, "Cossacks from the Georgian region of Guria headed by Colonel Cody are in London now taking the city by storm. Today they performed at Windsor, in front of Her Majesty, Queen Victoria." This was not the

Data Kadjaia (courtesy Buffalo Bill Museum and Grave, Golden, Colorado).

Gurians' and first encounter with the Queen, however. It is known that in the second half of the 19th century, Her Majesty Queen Victoria invited Prince Dimitri Gurieli[14] for dinner, who came dressed in his native clothing and attracted much attention.

After the performance, the Wild West cast returned by special train to London. The season at Earl's Court closed on October 12, and the Wild West cast set sail on board the S.S. *Mohawk* on October 15. The Georgian riders sailed for home on the same day.

It wasn't the show's last performance in front of royal family members. In 1903, King Edward VII, Queen Alexandra, Princess Victoria, Prince and Princess Charles of Denmark, and three children of the Prince of Wales all enjoyed Buffalo Bill's Rough Riders performing at the Olympia pavilion.

> A tearoom, hung with old gold velvet and decorated with flowers, was at the back of the special royal box, and there the King and Queen and their party had tea at the performance's close. They afterward visited the Indian camp, where Colonel Cody was presented to them. Cody and Burke then escorted the royal party through the settlement, where the Rough Riders were drawn up in a double line.[15]

Buffalo Bill Cody's Wild West toured Great Britain several times. They also visited Scotland, for the second time in 1904. Tom F. Cunningham wrote about the "Cossacks":

> The squadron of riders billed in the official programme as "Cossacks, from the Caucasus of Russia" were increased to a full score for the 1904 season. Their truly amazing exhibition of horsemanship surpassed anything else to be seen in the show for agility, originality and daring. This unique brand of equestrianism combined a wild dash and individuality of style with the seemingly irreconcilable element of discipline.[16]

A newspaper detailed one incredible maneuver:

> With his horse at full gallop he swoops down and picks up a handkerchief from the ground, holds fast by the saddle and seems to float in the air alongside, swings himself back to his seat and throwing his feet straight up in the air rests on his shoulders, or head, on the saddle, and finally crossing his stirrups over the saddle stands upright with his toes in them, and all this without diminishing his headlong pace.[17]

As usual, various newspapers ran unbelievable stories about the "Russian Cossacks":

5. On Her Majesty's Service

Spectators at the Buffalo Bill's Wild West Exhibition may have noted the leader of the Cossack riders and, at the same time, have little suspected that the horseman was a Prince according to the laws of Circassia. His name is Prince David Kadjaia, and among the Cossack tribes a man is entitled to a patent of nobility should he possess inherited land. Kadjaia, however, is more proud of being the possessor of the Cross of St. George, which in the Russian Empire corresponds to the Victoria Cross, than he is of his exalted title. This distinction was conferred by the Emperor Alexander II as a reward for the Cossack's bravery at the Siege at Kars, during the Russo-Turkish War. At that time Kadjaia was a sergeant in the Cossack battalion. He is of a roving, restless disposition and for the past few years has commanded the Cossack band who form an interesting feature in the programme presented by Col. Cody.[18]

Cody and his company arrived in New York October 24, marking the end of the show's four-year tour of Europe. The following season was to be the biggest and best.

6. The Georgian Cossacks

As mentioned before, the Wild West show organizers initially paid little attention to the riders' origin, identifying them Russian Cossacks, Caucasus Cossacks, Circassians or even Caucasian Jews. "Cossacks perched on their high saddles looked like a section of Brownsville, untrimmed whiskers having a Hebraic suggestion to the American eye. Buffalo Bill himself rode behind the Cossacks."[1]

On June 13, 1892, *Moskovskie Vedomosti* reprinted an article by Alex Kinloch from *The Army & Navy Gazette,* in which he reported

> that the eleven Russian horsemen … are not Cozacks [sic] … I spent a great part of twenty years in Russia among the troops, and I have seen dances and have heard the songs of the Russian soldiers and Cozacks, and I speak, therefore, from my impressions as an eye-witness. On being questioned by me the men at the show confessed that they were not Cozacks, and said they were Lezgins [a tribe in the Caucasus], and they were not, and never had been, in any military service. Their peculiar accent and unmistakable gestures, as well as certain movements in their dance, created a strong suspicion in me that they are Caucasian Jews.

This revelation was confirmed by the *Saturday Review,* which categorically identified them as Georgians. These revelations made not the slightest dent in the Georgians' popularity with the general public, for whom the precise ethnic origin of these strange riders remained a secondary consideration.[2]

The Georgians were less than happy, though. Tedo Sakhokia, who bumped into them in Paris in 1903, quoted them as saying: "It's a disgrace. No matter how hard we try to explain that we are from Georgia, they don't get the message and call us 'Cossacks' and don't even want to recognize the fact that we are actually Georgians."[3] Not surprising that no one had any information about Georgians and Georgia, since at that time Georgia was part of the Russian Empire and each of its citizens implied to be a Russian. "I asked my fellow American," wrote an unknown rider in his diary, "Do you know where Black Sea is?" "No," he replied. "Caucasus?" "No!" "Georgia?" "No," he said once again…

6. The Georgian Cossacks

"Then what do you know for Christ sake? How did they managed to build such a wonderful country?!" On July 17, 1897, the *Hamilton Spectator* reported:

> The Cossacks are a jolly crowd off duty. The writer was introduced to their chief by Mr. Fellows, the manager. He is called Prince "Lucas," and is said to be a prince in his own country, though the name is probably an Anglicized version. He can talk English a little, and is very proud of it. He was accompanied by another Cossack, a fine looking fellow with a pointed beard, who carries a Russo-English dictionary around with him... Prince "Lucas" gave the writer a lot of information about the Cossacks, and was careful to explain that they are not Russians, but Georgians, from the Caucasus. Mr. Fellows said: "This gentleman is a writer for the newspapers," and he proceeded to go through the form of writing on his hand. "Oh, yeez," said Prince "Lucas," smiling intelligently, "he a correspondez."

Pen and Pencil (July 16, 1892) described one day in the "Cossacks'" life in Kensington, England.

> They all talk Russian, not fluently, and not with the proper accent, and even the chief [Ivane Makharadze] among these princes shakes his head and shows his glittering white teeth as, with a slightly contemptuous smile, he says, "No, I don't know it well. We talk our own language, the Georgian dialect." ["They speak principally Georgian," announced the *Star*, May 31, 1892]. [The Georgian language] "sounds like gutturals, varying in nothing except the tone in which they are pitched. The Georgian language does not seem to be musical; and you wonder as you listen how it may sound when the Cossacks mother sings to her infant that loveliest of cradle songs...."

Georgian and its sister languages Mingrelian, Laz, and Svan, form the Kartvelian language family (Kartveli means Georgian). On June 25, 1995, *The New York Times* suggested that "language families like Afro-Asiatic, which includes Arabic and Hebrew, the Kartvelian languages of the south Caucaus and the Dravidian languages concentrated in southern India, all are descendants of Nostratic, which was spoken more than 12, 000 years ago." The Georgian language "like most of the many Caucasian languages, is not related (at least not closely or demonstrably) to any on earth."[4] With the Russians and other Slavs, the Georgians have no relationship whatsoever. The earliest extant Georgian inscriptions date from the 5th century, and manuscripts survive from the seventh century, while the first Georgian book was printed in the 17th century.

Later, many riders became fluent in English. When the Soviets ruled Georgia, in the late 20s, Kolkhoz (a collective farm owned by the Soviet

Georgian Trick Riders in American Wild West Shows

Unknown Georgian horsemen in England, circa 1904.

state) authorities hired English and American advisors, mostly females, for tea plantations in Lanchkhuti, Guria. Naturally Georgians threw a party in honor of the guests. Everybody enjoyed themselves eating traditional Georgian meals and drinking wine. The tamada (toastmaster) was former rider Panteleimon Tsintsadze. He was very handsome man, and one American woman exclaimed in English "What a handsome guy!" Tsintsadze, who knew English well, didn't react, but when he pronounced the toast in good English, it was like bomb explosion. They didn't suspect that there were a lot of English-speaking Georgians in the small town of Lanchkhuti.

"It is probable that audience members were satisfied that the performers were Russian and that they could present a colorful and exciting as part of the show," wrote author Sarah J. Blackstone.[5] Audiences wanted to see different kinds of presenters, and clever businessman Buffalo Bill Cody decided to involve representatives of other nations in his show and solved this problem at once: Georgian peasants became Cossacks, Sioux Indians became Cheyennes or Apaches, all Native Americans were chiefs in the show, all Asiatic (Chinese or Indian) women were princesses, army horsemen were colonels, etc. "I can put a pair of boots, a big hat, and a red shirt on any man, call him a cowboy," Cody once

6. The Georgian Cossacks

told a reporter, "but I cannot dress anyone up and call him an Indian."[6] It is known that in the show, Native Americans sometimes pretended as cowboys. Even Cody had fabricated his own past and sometimes inserted himself into Wild West history. According to some sources, Buffalo Bill did not ride for the Pony Express in 1860—he was still at school in Leavenworth most of that year—and neither did he work for the Kansas Pacific Railway as a buffalo hunter in 1867, during which time he later claimed to have killed 4,280 buffalo; the actual total was considerably less. Indeed, "This is the West, sir. When the legend becomes fact, print the legend" (from *The Man Who Shot Liberty Valance,* directed by John Ford, 1962).

Some newspapers carefully investigated the origin of the Georgian riders: "Prince Ivan Makharadze is in command of the 10 great strapping, black-bearded fellows from the Georgian village of Ozurgeti."[7] "They are not Cossacks at all, but one of the Caucasian tribes from the government of Kutais. Their proper designation is Kafkaskia Grousini—that is, Georgians of the Caucasus."[8]

From the beginning and throughout their career, the newspapers continued to print stories about "Russian Cossacks."

> Prince Lucca, whose cleverness as a horseman is in keeping with his reputation as one of the most intrepid of the Czar's Cossack fighters, will head the company of wild Cossack riders. Strictly speaking, the Cossacks are not a Wild West feature. More appropriately the Wild East. They are introduced in the performance, however, for the purpose of giving the audience an idea of the method of riding in vogue in the Russian Steppes, as compared with the method common to the American cowboy, the riders of Mexico, and the wild horsemen of the Indian reservations.[9]

Regarding this confusion, it might be worth mentioning that Thomas Oliver and the show's organizers were responsible for creating this initial mystery in the media by declaring that the riders came from the southern part of the Russian Caucasus, where the Cossack family in Lord Byron's narrative poem "Mazeppa" came from. Major John Burke, Buffalo Bill's press agent, embellished the Georgian riders' tales, much as Ned Buntline had in creating the Buffalo Bill image.[10]

Here is one example:

> These Cossacks, in the picturesque garb of the Caucasus, form the latest acquisition of the Wild West. They are a troop of "Cossacks of the Caucasian Line," under the command of Prince Ivan Makharadze.
> The Prince and his comrades, it is interesting to the public to know, belong

to the same branch of the great Cossack family, the Zaporogians, immortalized by Byron's "Mazeppa." Mazeppa was the hetman, or chief, of the Zaporogian community of the Cossacks of the Ukraine.

When Byron's famous hero came to grief at the battle of Poltava, the Cossacks fled to the Crimea, then Turkish territory, to avoid the vengeance of Peter the Great. Subsequently they were deported to the Kuban, and settled along the river as military colonists, to defend the Russian frontier against the marauding tribes of the Caucasus.

On this dangerous frontier the qualities of horsemanship that made the name of Mazeppa and his warlike followers household words throughout the whole of Europe became still further developed in the following generations, so that the Kuban Cossacks quickly became, in many respects, the most remarkable riders in the world.

On their lithe steppe horses, as fierce and active as themselves, they proved themselves more than worthy of their sires. During the heroic struggle of the Circassian mountaineers to maintain their independence against Russia, the sons of Mazeppa's Zaporogians were found to be the only Cossacks sufficiently skillful to cope with Schamyl's wild mountain horsemen on equal terms. The Don Cossacks were lancers, and the Circassians quickly learned to dodge within their guard, and cut them down, they being among the most expert swordsmen in the world.

But the descendants of Mazeppa's Cossacks were equally expert with the sword, and so, in the matter of arms, as of horsemanship, met the enemy on equal terms. For many years the Cossacks of the Caucasian line were engaged in a perpetual border warfare with the Circassian tribes. Their fighting was a series of little cavalry combats, surprises and raids, similar to the American Indian frontier wars, the finest school for the development of military horsemanship the world has seen since the days of Saladin and Coeur-de-Lion. Graduates from this fierce, wild school of saddle and saber, the Cossacks of the Caucasian line have long enjoyed the reputation of being the flower of that vast horde of irregular cavalry, the Cossack military colonies that have been planted along the southern frontier of the Russian Empire, from the Crimea to the Chinese border on the Pacific.

Circassian blood plainly crops out in the Cossacks of the Buffalo Bill Wild West arena. Indeed, some of them look the Circassian, even more than the Cossack. The infusion of Circassian, Georgian and Mingrelian blood began with stirring drama of strife and romance in the days of Schamyl.[11] Part of the policy of Russia was the suppression of the trade in Circassian beauties for the harems of Turkey, then carried on in small Turkish vessels in the Black Sea. A Cossack coastguard service was organized for the purpose, consisting of fleets of rowboats concealed in the creeks and inlets of the Caucasian coast, whence they could pounce out on the slave ships.

The vessels usually contained from forty to fifty Circassian, Georgian and Mingrelian slave girls, lovely creatures selected for the harems of the Sultan

6. The Georgian Cossacks

In center, Panteleimon Tsintsadze.

and the wealthy Pashas of Constantinople. The slaves thus captured were given to the Cossacks of the Kuban for wives; hence the sons and daughters of Schamyl's fierce opponents are as much Circassian as Cossack. The combination is a "strain" of horsemanship that has produced startling and unique results in the form of riders capable of really marvelous feats of a kind never before seen outside of Russia. Visitors to the Wild West who have marveled at the skill of the Indians and the Cowboys with the bucking mustangs will marvel anew at the striking performances of these descendants of the famous "Mazeppa."[12]

Even the riders boasted that they were awarded medals for bravery, but it was a con, of course.

The Cossacks with the Wild West are in the charge of Prince David Kadjaia, whose home and native land is in the Caucasus. He is a distinguished soldier and wears several medals for bravery on the field of battle. He has the cross of St. George bestowed upon him at the battle of Khartoum, and also wears a medal for bravery at Plevna during the campaign of 1877–78. He is a tall, fine-looking man, wearing a heavy full beard, and is very intelligent and well educated; although he can only speak a few words of English, but appears to understand simple questions asked of him in English, quite well.[13]

Or this brilliant example of a fictional story:

A full blooded native of the plains of Tartary, with an ancestry that can be traced in direct line to the kings who ruled most of Central Asia ... Luka,

Georgian Trick Riders in American Wild West Shows

son of Lon, is the first prince to visit St. Louis.... Luka held a commission from the Czar in the recent Russian-Japanese war ... having come up from the forbidden land of Tibet ... he has been in the service of the Grand Llama.... He is a soldier of fortune ... Pawnee Bill's agents met him in Port Arthur.... He enlisted a score of Cossacks from his former troop.[14]

As I mentioned before, Georgian horsemen mostly were ordinary farmers, and none are known ever to have been in military service.

Other newspapers went even further, such as *The Hutchinson Leader*, which ran an article on July 24, 1908.

The Cossacks were the real thing, right from the Czar's army. Splendid horsemen and brave fighters, they are also fierce and cruel. They were members of the same regiment that charged upon a throng of men, women and children in the streets of St. Petersburg two years ago and shot and sabered, murdered a thousand.

Russians pogroms against the Jewish people, as executed by Cossacks, helped make them widely recognizable and popular, if fierce heroes, "semi-civilized ... warriors from the Russian Empire."[15] "Pogrom is a Russian word meaning 'to wreak havoc, to demolish violently.' ... 'Pogrom' came into common usage with extensive anti–Jewish riots that

Georgian horsemen, France, circa 1904.

swept Ukraine and southern Russia in 1881–1884, following the assassination of Czar Alexander II."[16]

The image of bad guys followed Cossacks even after Wild West shows' popularity had declined—they were bad guys on the silver screen also. In John Ford's *Cheyenne Autumn* (1964), Sr. First Sergeant Wichowski (Mike Mazurki) said: "I'm a Pole.... A Cossack is a man on a horse.... Now he kills Poles just because they're Poles. Like we're trying to kill Indians just because they're Indians. I was proud to be an American soldier, but I ain't proud to be a Cossack!"

The *New York Times* (September 24, 1895) described an incident.

> Bernard Bernes, a Hebrew, eighteen years old ... was perched on an awning post watching the parade of Buffalo Bill's show when the affair occurred. In the parade was a Russian Cossack mounted. As the Cossack passed the point where Bernes was, the latter shouted something at him. The Cossack reined in his horse, dashed into the crowd to a spot near the post, and began to ply his long, heavy whip across Bernes's back. Bernes was lightly clothed, and the heavy lash brought blood. A number of citizens interfered and forced the Cossack to cease beating the Hebrew. The Cossack has not been arrested.

The Czar's Cossacks' pogroms against the Jews in Russia apparently incited the young man to shout insults at the Georgian rider.

It must be mentioned that there is no other country except Georgia where the tradition of the relationship between Jews and other Georgians has no signs of anti–Semitism. Historical documents clearly show that Georgian-speaking Jews are one of the oldest surviving Jewish communities in the world. They and Georgians had equal economic and legal rights, and they peacefully coexisted together for approximately 2,600 years.

In 1911, an employee of Kit Carson's Buffalo Ranch Wild West, cowboy Milton David Hinkle, wrote an article describing his show days and a story linked with Russian Cossacks and a Jew. Milton wrote about the show's thieves and describes in detail how one of these tricks worked. The trick that Milton describes concluded when the man who had been robbed received help from the "Russian Cossacks" who worked in the show.

> The show had ten to twelve Russian Cossacks working, doing Russian riding in the show, and when the Jew started rattling off in Russian, telling the Cossacks all that had happened, they sided in with him. After a lot of Russian conversation, the Jew left the lot and we did not see him anymore that night. However, upon our arrival in the next town, the first person I saw was the Jew, and he was with the Cossacks. We were ready to leave the lot for parade

Unknown trick rider.

when I saw the Jew and the Cossacks once more, and this time they were talking unless you give him back his money, eight hundred dollars, we will tell the cops. I rode up just in time to hear the leader of the Cossacks say, "We refuse to work unless you give him back his money, eight hundred dollars, or we will tell the cops all about what is going on. The legal adjuster took a piece of paper from his pocket and had the Jew sign his name to it. He then handed the Jew five one-hundred-dollar bills, and the Jew was satisfied. He admitted later that he had lost only four hundred dollars and said the experience was worth it.[17]

7. Master of the Rough Riders

This is how the Georgian newspaper *Tsnobis Purtsely* described the Wild West show.

> The American circus named after its owner Buffalo Bill is not a circus but an ethnographical exhibition; the people of various nations, clad in their national outfit and ammunition, enact scenes, sometimes in a field, at home, or during battles. Imagine a circus, where more than 200 riders are incorporated into the battle scenes. The stage is so huge that riders look like ants, and for that reason, organizers employ a "shouter" though even he fails to communicate the messages to the public. The Circus can seat 10 to 12 thousand people. Everything is eccentric; first American Indians, exactly like those described in James Fennimore Cooper's books, appear in the arena accompanied by their families and demonstrating their family rites. They are dressed in colored clothes; they walk with their heads high and have peculiar smiles on their faces.

From 1893, electric power was added to the shows for the help in night performances. Buffalo Bill had started lighting his arenas with Thomas Edison's electric lights. He was also using generators and dynamos.

Before the show, the parade got under way and was witnessed by thousands of men, women, and children lining the streets. Local newspaper *Washtenaw Times* commented:

> Buffalo Bill and his big show arrived in the city early this morning in 46 cars over the Lake Shore & Michigan Southern from Adrian. Col. Cody occupied his private Pullman and the whole outfit was sidetracked in the Michigan Central yards. The procession started at 9:30 o'clock and was headed by Buffalo Bill himself in a handsome spider with a footman behind and a pair of fine speckled white horses in front. After passing up Adams Street and down Cross over the river, the parade turned into River Street and then back on Congress, the grounds where the exhibition occurred.[1]

In the parade participated the famous "Congress of Nations"—the long lines of Germans, English, Cubans, Turkish and Transvaal Rough Riders. "The Cossacks [had] their long grey coats, fur hats, and high saddles. These riders were followed with intense interest. Even then they were representatives of a nation which considered itself the prospective competitor of this country."[2]

After the parade came the cowboy band, opening the show with a stirring overture. The Indians, Mexicans, Arabs, Gauchos, Cossacks, cowboys, the cavalry of the different nations, and all the riders came in, all riding at a dead run. After all were drawn up in line, Buffalo Bill Cody himself rode on his magnificent white horse, raised his hat, and under an ovation of thousands introduced the Rough Riders of the World to the public.

The Buffalo Bill's Wild West show 1893 event program announced:

OVERTURE, "Star Spangled Banner," Cowboy Band, Wm. Sweeney, Leader.

1—GRAND REVIEW introducing the Rough Riders of the World and Fully Equipped Regular Soldiers of the Armies of America, England, France, Germany, and Russia.

2—MISS ANNIE OAKLEY, Celebrated Shot, who will illustrate her dexterity in the use of Fire-arms.

3—HORSE RACE between a Cowboy, a Cossack, a Mexican, an Arab, and an Indian, on Spanish-Mexican, Broncho, Russian, Indian and Arabian horses.

4—PONY EXPRESS. The former Pony Post rider will show how the Letters and Telegrams of the Republic were distributed across the immense Continent previous to the Railways and the Telegraph.

5—ILLUSTRATING A PRAIRIE EMIGRANT CROSSING THE PLAINS. Attack by marauding Indians repulsed by "Buffalo Bill," with Scouts and Cowboys.

6—A GROUP OF SYRIAN AND ARABIAN HORSEMEN will illustrate their style of Horsemanship, with Native Sports and Pastimes.

7—COSSACKS, of the Caucasus of Russia, in Feats of Horsemanship, Native Dances, etc.

8—JOHNNY BAKER, celebrated Young American Marksman.

9—A GROUP OF MEXICANS from Old Mexico will illustrate the use of Lasso, and perform various Feats of horsemanship.

10—RACING BETWEEN PRAIRIE, SPANISH AND INDIAN GIRLS.

12—MILITARY EVOLUTIONS by a Company of the Sixth Cavalry of the United States Army: a Company of the First Guard Uhlan Regiment of his Majesty King William II, German Emperor, popularly known as the "Potsdamer Reds"; a Company of French Chasseurs (Chasseurs a Cheval de la Garde Republique Franciaise); and a Company of the 12th Lancers (Prince of Wales' Regiment) of the British Army.

13—CAPTURE OF THE DEADWOOD MAIL COACH BY THE INDIANS, which will be rescued by "Buffalo Bill" and his attendant Cowboys.

N.B.—This is the identical old Deadwood Coach, called the Mail Coach,

7. Master of the Rough Riders

which is famous on account of having carried the great number of people who lost their lives on the road between Deadwood and Cheyenne 18 years ago. Now the most famed vehicle extant.

14—RACING BETWEEN INDIAN BOYS ON BAREBACK HORSES.

15—LIFE CUSTOMS OF THE INDIANS. Indian Settlement on the Field and "Path."

16—COL.W.F. CODY, ("Buffalo Bill"), in his Unique Feats of Sharpshooting.

17—BUFFALO HUNT, as it is in the Far West of North America—"Buffalo Bill" and Indians. The last of the only known Native Herd.

18—THE BATTLE OF THE LITTLE BIG HORN, Showing with Historical Accuracy the scene of CUSTER'S LAST CHARGE.

19—SALUTE.

CONCLUSION.

On April 20, 1898, German-born American inventor Emile Berliner recorded Buffalo Bill Cody's speech "Sentiments on the Cuban Question," where Cody supported intervention to protect U.S. interests in Cuba. This 98-second recording makes it difficult to hear what famous showman says. But at the end of the recording, Buffalo Bill clearly pronounces: "Ladies and Gentlemen, permit me to introduce to you a Congress of the Rough Riders of the World!" As Juti Winchester, an assistant professor of history at Fort Hays State University in Kansas, comments, "That's what Buffalo Bill was really all about: performance—in service to the West and the horseback cultures of world."[3] During the war campaign in Cuba, Theodore Roosevelt had asked Buffalo Bill to join the Rough Riders when he first organized that regiment. Unable to go himself, Cody had sent several of his best marksmen. In the final record of the diary of an unknown rider, we read:

> Now America is at war with Spain, on the island of Cuba. I red in the newspaper that Roosevelt gathered all the brave riders and drove them to fight. I saw Roosevelt in New York.... Now I think to join them, but have not decided yet. I'm a good rider and a marksman, but Iris (his wife or girlfriend) refusing to let me go....

We don't know what actually happened to this man. Afterward, Cody in his Wild West show staged the charge up San Juan Hill and played Colonel Roosevelt himself.[4] Wild West hired 16 veterans of Roosevelt's regiment for the show, so for the 1902 performance in Santa Barbara, the "Battle of San Juan Hill" was the featured closing spectacle, replacing "Custer's Last Stand."

Georgian Trick Riders in American Wild West Shows

Before television, radio, or the film industry, traveling exhibitions were the biggest form of entertainment most people came across. At the same time, newspapers and novels told of the adventures Americans experienced settling the western half of the country: exploring, fighting the natives, hunting, and building communities. The Wild West show

Unknown Georgian on parade.

merged the entertainment of the circus with the adventure of the new west and brought it to crowds of the eastern United States and beyond. The stars of the Wild West shows were as famous as world leaders and military heroes, or even more so. America's first entertainer, P. T. Barnum, conducted a "Grand Buffalo Hunt," complete with Native American dancers, in New Jersey in 1843. Exhibitions of cowboy skills began attracting spectators to Santa Fe as early as 1847. From these days the Wild West show gradually evolved, especially in the mind of Buffalo Bill Cody.

Major "Arizona" John M. Burke (in reality he was not a major and had no obvious connection to Arizona), general manager and chief press agent for Buffalo Bill's Wild West, recalled how the Wild West had developed:

> The original idea of the Wild West performance ... grew out of the misconception which Col. Cody saw the East had of the Indian and the cowboy. Cody went on the stage in 1872 as an actor of cowboy parts. He soon saw that the regions of civilization had an entirely erroneous idea of what the Indian was, what life on the plains was, and what the people who lived that life were like.
> Nate Salsbury, whose life had been spent on the stage and in the amusement business, had made some investments about this time in Montana. He became interested in Western history, and he saw the possibilities of a Wild West exhibition. He became acquainted with Indians. He saw that some of the robes they wore were richer and more carefully made than the garments which graced many a throne. The Indian then had plenty of beaver and his pick of buffaloes. But the East knew little of him.
> Cody and Salsbury talked the matter over. They decided to make an experiment. So on the Fourth of July, 1881, they gave their first trial performance. It was at North Platte, Ne., and a tremendous crowd gathered to see it. Cody had collected buffaloes, wild horses, cowboys, Mexicans, and about a hundred Indians. There was great doubt expressed whether when this strange aggregation came together it would not be a death-dealing affair. But instead it proved a great success.
> In 1883, after long preparation, a season was arranged, and the Wild West made its first tour. It traveled across the continent, playing generally on race tracks and at fairs. It was a heterogeneous organization, but wholly American, and it gave a remarkably accurate idea of the life on the plains. The exhibition was designed from the first to be a series of pictures.
> It was at first thought that so much shooting would cause great difficulty. It was said that horses would be frightened, women and children would be terrified. It was then that Col. Cody devised the idea of graduating the excite-

ment. Miss Annie Oakley was secured. She comes on very early in the performance. She starts very gently, shooting with a pistol. Women and children see a harmless woman there, and they do not get worried. Gradually she increased the charge in her rifles until at the last she shoots with a full charge. Thus, by the time the attack on the stagecoach comes the audience is accustomed to the sound of shooting, and in all the history of the Wild West there has never been a horse frightened sufficiently to run away at any of our outdoor performances.

For several years we carried only 200 people, while now we take 600. It was very difficult to get Indians in those days, because many of the tribes were at any time liable to break out in fighting. Their chiefs objected to their going. And then they themselves were afraid. It was a wonderful experience in the lives of these redmen when they appeared before crowds of 10,000 palefaces and saw that they were not massacred. They went back and told their fellow-redmen about it, and it has all had a tremendous influence in pacifying them.

In 1886 we commenced carrying our own equipment. In that year we established an arena at Erastina, Staten Island, where we showed for a whole summer. We put down four miles of railroad track there and spent $8,000 on a dock. We operated sixteen steamboats in New York Harbor, taking passengers from New York, Brooklyn, Hoboken, Jersey City, Elizabethport, Long Island City, and all other points in the harbor down to Staten Island. The experiment was a wonderful success.

That year we first showed at Madison Square Garden. We gave a representation of the primeval forest. We had a panoramic scene 300 feet by 55. We showed the burning prairie, and we invented the wind machine to exhibit a tornado on the prairie. The wind manufactured was strong enough to blow the stage coach a considerable distance across the Garden.[5]

In the late 19th and early 20th centuries, Buffalo Bill's Wild West show, one of the most successful outdoor traveling shows in American history, toured the United States and Europe, playing to enormous crowds.[6]

Attending the Wild West show often seemed like an initiation into living popular Western history. The scenes and narratives enacted on stage were dramatic and colorful reenactments of famous incidents such as the "Attack on the Deadwood Stage Coach," "Attack on a settler's Cabin," "Great Hold-Up," "Bandit Hunters of the Union Pacific," "Attack on an Emigrant Train," "Custer's Last Stand," and so forth. After seeing the show, the author of *Huckleberry Finn*, Mark Twain, wrote Cody, "I have now seen your Wild West show two days in succession, enjoyed it thoroughly. It brought back to me the breezy, wild life of the Rocky

Mountains and stirred me like a war song. The show is genuine—cowboys, vaqueros, Indians, stagecoaches, costumes, the same as I saw them in the frontier years ago."[7]

Buffalo Bill promoted his displays as educational exhibits and not shows—in fact, it was called the "Wild West," never the "Wild West Show." Careful to distinguish his spectacle from the circus, Colonel Cody kept the word "show" out of title. Audiences also were cautioned to remember that the difference between a Wild West show and a circus was that in the circus, performers did things they learned only for the circus, while Wild West stars performed feats which are learned for quite other purposes, and, for the most part, for some important purpose. "When we learned to ride with Buffalo Bill, there were no chutes to make it easy for a rider to mount a bucking bronc. We snubbed down the brute, maybe biting his ear, till a rider got aboard; then we turned him loose. The rider stayed until the bronc stopped bucking—or the rider lost his seat. There were no fancy pick-offs," said Wild West show employee Glenn (Shorty) Kischko in an interview.[8] For example, to show an Indian massacre of a wagon train, a wagon-train bedded down for the night, with the wagons drawn up in a semicircle. It was a night show, and all lights were extinguished. In the distance were faint sounds to signify the approach of the Sioux Indians. Out of darkness, burning arrows flashed into the tarpaulin of the covered wagons. The tarps, having been sprayed with kerosene, burst into flames, and the Indians rode in, painted and whooping.

"Women screamed and scampered for safety in the light of the burning wagons. In order to make the children scream during the attack, mothers pinched their kids to produce genuine crying...."[9]

As Cody's future companion and showman Pawnee Bill (his successful Pawnee Bill's Historic Wild West began touring in 1888, and two decades later the "Two Bills" merged their shows) put it, "All is real. Everything is a fact.... It is an object lesson in the story of a great people, a narrative told and illustrated by themselves."[10]

The Wild West show featured a multicultural company that included riders from five continents and strangely diverse ethnic groups. Everything from American Indians, cowboys and cowgirls, and Mexican vaqueros to Boers, gauchos, Japanese "samurai," cavalrymen from the United States, Germany, France, and the United Kingdom, and Cossacks were represented. Others would be added as the years passed by. Journalist Opie Read gives a fine description of the show:

> Morse made two worlds touch the tips of their fingers together. Cody has made the warriors of all nations join hands.
>
> In one act we see the Indian, with his origin shrouded in history's mysterious fog: the cowboy—nerve-strung product of the New world: the American soldier, the dark Mexican, the glittering soldier of Germany, the dashing cavalryman of France, the impulsive Irish dragoon, and the strange, swift spirit from the plains of Russia, the Cossacks. Marvelous theatric display, a drama with scarcely a word—Europe, Asia, Africa in panoramic whirl—and yet as individualized as if they had never left their own country.[11]

An interesting quote can be found in the diary of an unknown Gurian rider:

> They have brought some men from Australia. They are completely black with coal-black hair; they use a very strange wooden arm, which they call a boomoorang [sic]. It is flat and crooked, and when you throw it, it flies back to you.... They use it for hunting. One of the showmen asked them to give him the boomoorang, because he wanted to throw it himself. The Australian gave it to him, but warned him to be very careful. The showman threw it in very brave manner. It flew away, but he was not able to catch it when it flew back. It hit him in the face and, while he did not die, the silly guy was left for a long time with a tied-up jaw.

And this is the quote from *Brooklyn Daily Eagle* (April 24, 1894): "The Australian Blacks slapped their boomerangs together and looked pleased, the Cossacks lifted their eyebrows with an express of surprise."

William Frederick Cody, a.k.a. Buffalo Bill (1846–1917), was a frontiersman, hunter, scout, showman, and entrepreneur. In the end of the 19th and beginning of the 20th centuries, he was undoubtedly one of the most famous people on earth. Cody was born in LaClaire, Scott County, Iowa. Young Bill began his career as a Pony Express rider; at the age of 12, he claimed, he killed his first Native American. Bill attended short sessions of some schools, then in 1854 his family moved to Kansas, where his father was stabbed speaking for the Free State cause. He recovered, but three years later, in 1857, died.

After his father's death, the family drifted west, and during the American Civil War, Bill served as a Union scout. In 1867 Cody began hunting buffalo (reportedly he shot 4,280 of them) for Kansas Pacific work crews, thereby earning his nickname and reputation as an expert

7. Master of the Rough Riders

Wild West show cast, circa 1902.

shot. It must be noted that, before meeting with the so-called "Russian Cossacks," he already had provided service and entertainment to Grand Duke Alexis, the son of the Russian emperor Alexander II, who had arrived in the U.S. to tour North America. The Grand Duke had made his way to central Nebraska for his much anticipated participation in a buffalo hunt that would take place on his twenty-second birthday. Buffalo Bill Cody was to be his guide. The hunting party also included General Philip Sheridan and Colonel George Custer.

In his diary, Buffalo Bill wrote:

> The main thing was to give Alexis the first chance and the best shot at the buffaloes, and when all was in readiness, we dashed over a little knoll that had hidden us from view, and in a few minutes we were among them. Alexis at first preferred to use his pistol instead of a gun. He fired six shots from this weapon at buffaloes only twenty feet away from him, but as he shot wildly, not one of his bullets took effect. Riding up to his side and seeing

Georgian Trick Riders in American Wild West Shows

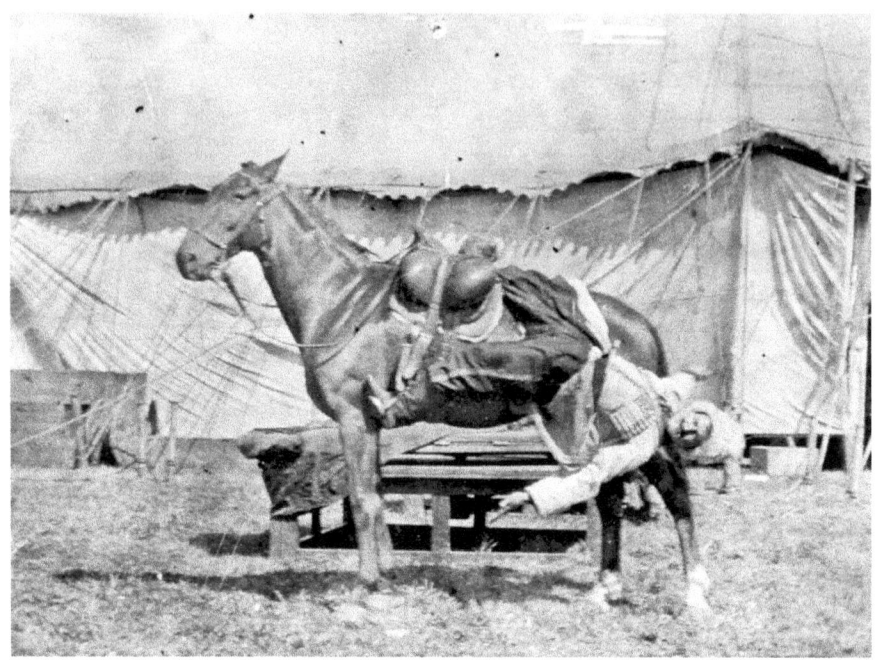

Ilarion Imnadze, United States, 1912.

that his weapon was empty, I exchanged pistols with him. He again fired six shots, without dropping a buffalo. Seeing that the animals were bound to make their escape without his killing one of them, unless he had a better weapon, I rode up to him, gave him my old reliable *Lucretia,* and told him to urge his horse close to the buffaloes.... "Now is your time," said I. He fired, and down went the buffalo.... Very soon the corks began to fly from the champagne bottles, in honor of the Grand Duke Alexis, who had killed the first buffalo.[12]

Buffalo Bill became one of only four civilian scouts to be awarded the Congressional Medal of Honor during the Indian Wars for valor in action.

Interestingly, Buffalo Bill Cody was mentioned in Georgian-American author and artist George Papashvily's bestseller *Anything Can Happen,* when he described his first day in Ellis Island:

> Zurabeg was an American citizen with papers to prove it, and a friend of Gaspadin [master in Russian] Buffalo Bill besides. This Zurabeg came first to America twenty years before as a trick show rider, and later he was boss

7. Master of the Rough Riders

cook on the road with Gospadin Buffalo Bill ... Buffalo Bill, an old friend of mine, has eaten thirty of my piroshkis [in Russian, baked or fried buns stuffed with a variety of filling].[13]

Probably the first live show exhibiting scenes from the West occurred in 1837, at George Catlin's Indian Gallery on Broadway in New York, when Native Americans shot arrows and performed war dances.[14] Buffalo Bill organized his first show, the "Old Glory Blow-out," in North Platte, Nebraska, on July 4, 1882.[15] When the show was launched in 1883, it was an immediate success. It was billed as "The Wild West, Hon. W. F. Cody and Dr. W. F. Carver's Mountain and Prairie Exhibition." Carver was Cody's business partner, but at the end of the season they separated. Soon Carver organized Wild America show and toured in Europe. According to Don Russell, during 1889–1891 the show performed in Berlin, Vienna, Budapest, Warsaw, Stockholm, St. Petersburg, and Moscow. Famed Russian journalist and writer Vladimir Gilyarovsky describes his meeting with Doc Carver's Wild America in Moscow. Once on the walls of Moscow, he wrote, appeared a huge billboard with giant letters on it: Wild America. That poster also mentioned the name of the famous entrepreneur, American cowboy Buffalo Bill, but certainly he wasn't here. (Buffalo Bill Cody's Wild West never played Russia.) Here came two dozen tattooed and painted Indians, with feathers on their heads, a few cowboys in straw hats and with the "murderous" spurs. Before him, as a representative of the press, cowboys performed several acts, included lassoing horses, trick riding, galloping, and vaulting. According to Gilyarovsky, it was mediocre entertainment, which was acted by cowboys and Indians with very serious faces. He was accustomed to life in the Don steppes and was an expert rider. He and his comrade Cossack mounted horses and did everything they did—repeated all their tricks in a much better way in front of them.

All were amazed and confused. The show's manager asked Gilyarovsky not to write anything about rehearsal. It was a short man who had brought this Wild America from abroad, which, according to him, had a great success in Europe.[16] But Wild America was not successful in Moscow.

Doc Carver returned to the United States in 1892 and continued his show through 1893. He was popular, proved himself a champion marksman, and invented the idea of horse-diving exhibitions, but he never became the household name that Buffalo Bill did.

In 1890, when the U.S. Census Bureau declared that the frontier, "the moving edge of settlement into the 'wilderness,'" officially no longer existed, half of a continent was explored, conquered and settled: "The frontier has gone, and with its going has closed the first period of American history."[17] During a meeting of the American Historical Association in Chicago, an event linked to the Chicago's World's Fair, historian Frederick Jackson Turner reiterated this information. In very different ways, Turner and Buffalo Bill Cody presented their versions of the frontier story to audiences. The Fair, and Chicago itself, symbolized the rise of the United States from an undeveloped rural colony to an industrial nation on the verge of becoming a colonial power itself. The ideas Turner and Cody offered to audiences in Chicago reflected a fascination with the past and a desire to use the past to explain how Americans could navigate the uncertain territory of the future. The Indians' role, historian Turner indicated in his famous thesis, was to get out of the way. As Turner addressed the gathered historians, Buffalo Bill was welcoming visitors to his Wild West, a vestige of that frontier.[18]

The capturing of the vanishing frontier world and cultures was deemed one of Cody's most important legacies. Buffalo Bill understand very early that the myth of the West could be manipulated for profit. Over its thirty-year run, Buffalo Bill's Wild West entertained millions and presented Cody's version of the lore of the American West.[19] Cody was skilled in the use of press and advertising. He knew what people wanted, he knew how to entertain them, because he liked them, was open to them, felt his kinship with them.[20] Buffalo Bill gave the show a dramatic narrative structure.

In the 1890s, Edison had filmed Wild West performers such as Annie Oakley shooting at targets, Mexicans demonstrating lasso throwing, Buffalo Bill himself, the Sioux Ghost Dance, the Buffalo Dance, the Indian War Council. As the century progressed, many Wild West shows had to compete with new entertainments, including motion pictures. Some of the shows' organizers started to make film versions of the shows, but despite these, most of the shows were in deep financial trouble due to declining attendance. At the turn of the 20th century, to avoid high costs and to add authenticity to his pictures, film producer and director Thomas Ince hired the Miller Brothers 101 Ranch Wild West Show, including many cowboys, horses, cattle, and a whole Sioux Indian tribe. The Wild West

7. Master of the Rough Riders

show contested with newborn cinema by offering the audience something that the film industry could not—the sounds of the Old West. But soon everything changed. Sound came to the cinema. The movies killed the Wild West show business, and Cody went into movies himself. He and Pawnee Bill formed the Buffalo Bill/Pawnee Bill Film Company and began producing a film that would reenact the Plains Indian wars of the late 1800s. In 1913, he made a Western *The Indian Wars* (directed by Theodore Wharton), where Cody reprised his own role as a scout on the western plains, the duel with Yellow Hand, the Battle of Summit Springs, etc., and focused on his efforts to achieve a truce in the Sioux Ghost Dance uprising. The film had no success, and the footage is lost. Before his death, in 1917, he played himself in *The Adventures of Buffalo Bill.* According to Joy S. Kasson, Buffalo Bill's Wild West left an indelible mark on the history of cinema. It established a vocabulary of incident and image that would become standard—even clichéd—to filmgoers around the world.[21]

Today the West that exists in the minds of Americans partially comes from Western movies and dime novels, but it's mostly the result of the way Buffalo Bill depicted it in his show. His Wild West had glam-

In center: **Dimitri Tsintsadze.**

orized the last frontier throughout much of the world, introducing the cowboy hero and opening the way for Western novels, movies, and television shows. But the extinct frontier continued to live in the minds and hearts of millions of Americans. Author J. Hoberman, speaking about Vietnam and the influence that was the Old West, frontier, and Western movies for several generations of Americans, especially for the youth of 60s, who were raised on Westerns (and at that time, eight of the top prime-time TV shows were Westerns), he noticed very accurately that "in the national dream life, Indochina was an extension of the Western frontier and Americans once again settlers, cavalrymen, schoolmarms, gunslingers, and marshals on a mission of protection and progress." And the enemy, meaning the Indians, was Vietnamese. American soldiers even swapped General Sheridan's famous slogan "The only good Indian is a dead Indian" and transformed it to "The only good Gook is a dead Gook," which was painted on their jackets.[22]

Buffalo Bill made millions, but he lost them in unwise investments. His Wild West had to be saved by Pawnee Bill, and the new joint show became "Buffalo Bill's Wild West and Pawnee Bill's Great Far East Combine."[23] On January 10, 1917, William Frederick Cody died, in bed and not in the arena, as he had feared.[24] At his death, Annie Oakley remembered, "His heart never left the great West. Whenever the day's work was done, he could always be found sitting alone watching the sinking sun, and at every opportunity he took the trail back to his old home."[25] The news of Buffalo Bill's death brought front-page headlines across the United States and tributes from far and wide.

"Buffalo Bill is gone;
Everyone knows the score.
Buffalo Bill and his Wild West Show
Won't be thrilling our hearts no more."[26]

This is how an unknown rider portrayed Buffalo Bill Cody:

> Everyone knows him in America; there are innumerable books written about him. These books describe his life and his buffalo hunting—that made him known as the Buffalo Bill. The books also describe how he transported the mail while working at the post office, how he fought the Indians and all other adventures that had happened to him. I enjoyed reading these books, but some of these stories did not seem true to me. How can a guy kill three Indians with one shot?

7. Master of the Rough Riders

The man who had much to do with making him famous and promoting his show was Ned Buntline, who was dramatizing the West in his stories and bringing the Indian into perspective with perception and sympathy. He had written a story showing Buffalo Bill killing Indians

Alexis Gogokhia-Georgian, left, and Luka Chkhartishvili (in Gurian dress) (courtesy Richard Alexis Georgian).

while he was a Pony Express rider. Once Buffalo Bill told the Wild West show member, Chief Red Fox, that "after reading the story I was afraid of myself ... killing three Indians with two shots. Frank Butler or his wife Annie Oakley could not have done that well, could they?" The stories Buntline wrote helped to bring Buffalo Bill into prominence as a dashing, glamorous figure as the West being industrialized and "civilized."[27]

A Gurian rider remembers:

> Buffalo Bill was a tall handsome man; he had long hair, wore moustache and a beard. He wore a leather suit.... A hat that the cowboys usually wear. He was a great horseback rider and a shooter. Once, when he performed before Queen of England and shooting glass balls from Winchester, Queen was so pleased that she said—This is a very good rifle and it's in a very good hands.

8. Alexis Gogokhia/Georgian

Buffalo Bill's Wild West gave birth to a variety of shows of varying quality in the United States. The Wild West shows could be found almost at every corner; there were around 117 recorded shows from this time. Even famous outlaws like Frank James and Cole Younger from Jesse James's gang launched a similar historical Wild West show after being rehabilitated in the beginning of the 20th century. It went bankrupt after a while but employed a number of Georgian riders. The *Lexington News* (September 3, 1903) wrote about Caucasian "Cossacks":

> The most exceptional cavalry soldiers of Europe are the "Caucasian Cossacks" of the Russian army. Blindly obedient to their officers, indifferent to danger and death, physical hardships and amazingly skillful in management of their tough, wiry steppe ponies—a breed closely akin to the mustangs—their representatives are among the most interesting personal exhibits in the Great Cole Younger and Frank James Wild West. It is not easy to view their fantastic feats on horseback in the light of military training, but perhaps that is their way of fighting and they are astonishers anyway.

One of those "cavalry soldiers" was a man of extraordinary fate, Alexis Gogokhia. He went to the United States in 1894, after being expelled with a so-called "Wolf Ticket"[1] from the Tbilisi Orthodox Theological Seminary along with 87 other students for leading a strike. Among other demands, the Georgian students requested a Georgian Language department and a discharge of some Russian teachers. Later many of these students became leaders in the socialist and communist revolution—Joseph Jugashvili, known as Stalin, Noe Jordania, Silibistro Jibladze, and many others.

When he arrived in New York, Alexis took a variety of random jobs and learned English. In 1897, when he contacted Luka Chkhartishvili and joined Buffalo Bill's Wild West show. Alexis once said, "I lived in New York City working in sweatshops as a sewing machine operator, then working in a drug store cleaning spittoons, and finally in a laundry pressing skirts. In the summer I was a horseback rider in wild west shows." He stayed with the show till the end of the 1899 season, and later, in 1900, he started working with his own group. That is the time when he changed his name to Alexis Georgian, although he also performed as Captain Georgian, Colonel Georgian, and Prince Georgian. It was said that by 1903–1905, he was in charge of practically every group of Georgians, Arab acrobats, and Turk performers in the United States.

In 1902, in Buckskin Bill's troupe of Rough Riders, Alexis and other Gurians were charging around the arena when Alexi Georgian's horse jarred a pole that held a kerosene lamp. The collision knocked the light from the pole, and an explosion followed. "Some of the burning fluid fell on the arm of Chief Georgian and the sleeve of his jacket was burned away. The performer was slightly burned about the arm and shoulder

Georgian trick riders, circa 1898 (courtesy Buffalo Bill Museum and Grave, Golden, Colorado).

also, but he did not lose control of his horse, which plunged furiously around the arena, but luckily held out until the end of his performance before having his injuries attended to. He was only slightly burned, but the wound gave him much pain."[2]

On April 21, 1904, *The Daily Oklahoman* reported the arrest of Alexis Georgian.

Left to right: **Alexander Murvanidze, Simon Oragvelidze and Pavle Makharadze.**

> Captain Alexis Georgian, the noted Cossack officer, who has for some time been connected with Buckskin Bill's Wild West show, was last night arrested by the police at the instance of some Turks who have been in his employ.
>
> While the charge made against Georgian is for vagrancy, it was made in order to detain the Russian and secure the payment of salaries alleged to be due to several Turks who have been with him. The Turks claim that they entered into a contract with Georgian for an engagement of two weeks, but have not received compensation and that Captain Georgian was paid $500 by the show management yesterday, then quit the company and was arranging to leave the city last night without notifying them of his going or paying them for their services.
>
> The Russian Officer was much put out at his detention and chafed over the fact that a personal bond was denied him. He said it was true that he had quit the show, but was going to join Campbell Brothers' show and intended to take fifteen people with him, including the complaining Turks, for whom, he claimed, he engaged lodging at the Compton hotel last night. His agent made an offer of settlement last night, but the Turks declined to make terms with him.

Alexis Georgian was released the next day.

In 1911, Alexis and his wife, Stella, became the owners, writers, and publishers of an English-language socialist newspaper, *The New Times*. Alexis opposed the 1914 war, and the U.S. government drove him out of the newspaper business by 1919 because of this opposition. Alexis was a founding member of the American Communist Party in September of 1919. It is interesting to note that Noe Jordania, the chairman of the government of Georgia's short-lived Democratic Republic between 1918–1921, invited him to take the post of Georgia's ambassador to the United States—a post that Gogokhia refused. According to documents preserved in the Czarist secret police "Okhranka" archive, in 1900, Gogokhia-Georgian, with a forged passport, arrived in Batumi and brought two boxes of revolutionary literature.[3]

He was persecuted by the U.S. government for his political views and sent to Ellis Island for deportation on the S.S. *Buford* in 1920, but a writ of habeas corpus from the Supreme Court removed him from this ship. He owned a bookstore, then a gas station and restaurant, and finally he returned to his roots and was a truck farmer. Alexis died in November 1940, still under a court order for deportation.

9. Coming to America

The Georgian newspaper *Iveria* (February 19, 1893) wrote, "Batumi: A person, who was entrusted to bring together a group of riders for the big Chicago World's Fair, has been in Guria. The group is already recruited and it consists of ten riders. All of them are brave fellows, well-armed. They arrived in Batumi on February 13 and will leave for America in a couple of days." On March 29, 1893, the Georgian trick riders, enlisted in Adam Forepaughs'[1] and Buffalo Bill's Wild West show, arrived in America for the first time by the ship *Chester*. They included: Prince Eristavi (Eristoff),[2] Alexander Tsintsadze, Giorgi Maqsimenishvili, Raphiel Tvaladze, Gaston Matitashvili, Michael Kobaladze, Prince Dimitri and Princess Frida Mgaloblishvili, plus five riders whose names are not identified: Andrew Tericuly, Lewis Stradizi, Michael Labladzi, Samuel Zilitzi, and Charles Raikini. (Fully deciphering the Georgian riders' names in the documents is challenging because the spelling was determined by the person writing the document. The spelling and pronunciation of their names puzzled the American newspaper reporters and the general public.)

The Pittsburgh Post (May 1, 1893) describes the Georgians:

> The Princess Dimitri [Frida Mgaloblishvili] is a bright, interesting and attractive young lady. She speaks five languages and can make herself understood in English. Prince Eristoff, one of the leading members of the troupe, is almost a giant in strength. He wears several medals and decorations that were presented to him by the Czar for bravery during the late Turko-Russian war.

The media continued to feed its readers with more stories about the Georgians. An extract from French *Petite Journal* reprinted by *Iveria* (#58, 1893) reports,

> Fifteen Caucasians visited our office today. All of them are the best in the business. These Caucasians, headed by Mr. Ercole, are about to depart to Chicago for a horse race that'll take place at the fair. Ercole seems to be an experienced manager. He's pretty sure that his riders are going to win the races. They have already sent the horses abroad. The head of the group is T.

Eristavi. Mr. Eristavi doesn't look different from his compatriots; he's dressed in a long coat, red jacket and leather hat, plus long pistols, and an ornamented saber and scabbard made of black leather. All of them are from the western region of Georgia. They have served in the Russian army and have witnessed numerous severe battles. Despite this, they don't speak Russian, the language they serve. They are a sight for sore eyes, these warriors! They look gloomy and peaceful at the same time. Deep dark eyes and long beards add charisma to their appearance. They sang a song that had a strange melody. Though the song was easy on the ear it had occasional bursts of howling. One listens to their singing and it instantly brings pictures of wastelands inhabited by aggressive warriors ready for a blood-bath. What a striking difference from our civilized and educated society. These arrogant and quiet barbarians are proud of their beauty and weapons but instantly become childish the moment they hear the sound of corks popping out of Champagne bottles.

The Pittsburg Dispatch (April 30, 1893) wrote:

The prince is accompanied by his wife, the Princess Dimitri [Frida], who is the only one of the Cossack troop who speaks English. She was educated in Paris and speaks with a French-Caucasian accent that is bewitching, but scarcely possible of reproduction in cold type. The princess is patriotic in support of the Cossack rough riders as the greatest horsemen of the world.

The Daily Tribune printed a conversation overheard between Dimitri Mgaloblishvili and Prince Eristavi after their ship arrived late, and the passengers missed their connections:

"Me thinks," said the proud Prince Eristoff, as he wrapped his fur-lined overcoat about his manly form, "the inhabitants of this village have not accorded unto us a royal welcome. Why should it be so?" Quote Dimitri, pensively, "It must need be a cold day when such a welcome is accorded. Do you observe that to-day is not especially chilly?"[3]

The Wild West show executives booked rooms for the Georgians at the Astor House, 225 Broadway, and notified the press a prince and princess would tour the city on Thursday. They visited the Pulitzer building, where from the dome they viewed the lower bay to Harlem. While in New York, Georgian trick riders visited the Mayor, who shook hands with each Georgian and then inspected their weapons.[4]

The horsemen from Georgia weren't the first Georgians who set foot on American soil. The first Georgian immigrants in the United States and Canada arrived as early as the 1820s. More began to come, especially from the poorer mountainous regions of Georgia, in the 1860s,

9. Coming to America

after the abolition of serfdom in the Russian empire. At the outbreak of the American Civil War, a considerable number of young military men from the Russian Empire offered their services to Abraham Lincoln and the Union. Among them was Prince Alexander Eristavi from Georgia. Alexander Eristavi didn't go to America voluntarily. He served in the regiment in his native Georgia. A Russian commander of his regiment never missed an opportunity to insult Georgia, its people, and the Georgian language, which he referred to as a dog's language. Once, Eristavi, who could no longer stand the abuse, slapped the commander in the face. Eristavi was arrested and handed over to the military tribunal. But somehow he managed to escape to neighboring Turkey, then to England, and in 1862, eventually to America. According to Eristavi's grandnephew, American-Georgian historian Alexandre Tarsaidze, Eristavi "fought with the North for the principles of the progress and freedom, although he was the owner of a tremendous estate in his native Georgia." His English was imperfect, and when called upon to explain why he had chosen to fight with the Union forces, he took a peach between his fingers: "Like this, the peach is so beautiful, and its skin with all those little hairs is

Left to right: **Ivane Baramidze, Luka Chkhartishvili, Nikoloz Antadze, unidentified, Ushangi Kvitaishvili, circa 1898.**

protection in the severest weather." Breaking the peach in half, holding the two pieces far apart, "But like this, it can withstand nothing! The peach will wither, it will turn ugly inside. Do not, I beg, let the country be happened to like a peach."[5] Eristavi fought under the command of Ivan Turchaninoff, better known by his Americanized name John Basil Turchin.

The American public was amazed and intrigued by "Cossacks'" outfit, especially by Frida's wardrobe.

> Another dress reform idea which was found to have practical demonstration with the Forepaugh shows is the comfortable walking dress, reaching to the knee. This is worn by the princess Dimitri, the only woman with the Cossacks, who was found upon the show grounds after the parade returned. It is the regular costume of her native land, and it sets off her trim figure in a manner to cause all women to envy her. Besides it allows perfect freedom of movement, and so cultivates that natural grace which all women seek to acquire. The princess wears high top boots with her short skirts, and the most violent opponent of a change in woman's dress could find no suggestion of immodesty in it.[6]

She wore breeches, very familiar to Americans from the late 18th century, and this is very odd that it made them surprised.

On April 10, 1893, a second group of riders arrived in New York. They included: Prince Ivane Makharadze, Luka Chkhartishvili, Qishvard Makharadze, Karaman Kalandarishvili, Ivane "Kid" Makharadze, Solomon Dgebuadze, Silibistro Makharadze, Giorgi Kalandarishvili, and Joseph Talakhadze. After the English triumph five months ago, Ivane and his troupe signed a new contract with Buffalo Bill to return and perform in Chicago. Luka Chkhartishvili was the only "Cossack" to return with him. Ivane spent the intervening months gathering a new troupe of riders and working with them. He gathered a new band that included his brothers, Paul and Silibistro, his two cousins, Kishvard and Ivane "Kid," brothers-in-law Karaman and Giorgi, and two other villagers.

The Georgian riders entered the "Gateway to America,"—Ellis Island.

> At five in the morning the engines stopped, and after thirty-seven days the boat was quiet.
> We were in America.
> I got up and stepped over the other men and looked out the porthole. Water and fog. We were anchoring off an island. I dressed and went on deck.
> Now began my troubles. What to do?[7]

9. Coming to America

That's how begins the book *Anything Can Happen* by George Papashvily. It is a funny and at the same time sad tale of one immigrant's new life in America. His book, written in 1945, reinforces our understanding of fears, problems, hopes, and experiences that all immigrants face when they move to a new country. His story begins at Ellis Island and continues through many memorable experiences of immigrating to America.

The other immigrant, Georgian army officer and refugee Simon Sidamon-Eristavi, who fled America after the Red Army invasion, describes his first day in America:

> After what seemed a very long time, we reached Ellis Island. Our hope was that somehow, during the stay on Ellis Island while we waited to be processed, we could eat. They told us that on Ellis Island they gave you good scrambled eggs and ham and things like that. Also, that you could wash there and bring yourself into some order....[8]

The ship's purser carefully prepared the Customs List of Passengers, listing each passenger by number, name, age, calling, native country, intended destination, and number of pieces of baggage they were traveling with.[9] Some records indicated the amount of money in their pocket: the S.S. *La Lorraine* (April 22, 1905) lists Georgian riders Kirile Khoperia, Ilarion Ebralidze, Mikheil Chkhartishvili, Bartlome Mshvidobadze, Serapion Imnadze, and Giorgi Chkonia; each of them had $20.

At first the immigration status of Georgian riders was listed as "rider," but it soon changed to "artist." Cody used his Cossacks and other foreign Rough Riders for his benefit in Chicago, but in July, United States Commissioner Hoyne said that Cody's company had violated the "Contract Labor Law." The contract labor law was passed to protect the workingmen in the United States from the influx of foreign laborers brought in by employers in conflict with labor organizations. Cody's managers were brought before the Commissioner and threatened with $1,000 fines per individual per day. Actors and singers were exempt from this law. Cody escaped this fine, and in coming years the immigration status of Cody's riders would be listed as "artists or professionals."[10]

Show agents helped arrange the payment of custom duties. Georgians gathered their equipment and boarded a ferry for New Jersey, where a train for Chicago departed. The train carried one hundred former U.S. Cavalry soldiers, ninety-seven Cheyenne, Kiowa, Pawnee, and

Sioux Indians, another fifty Cossacks and Hussars, 180 horses, eighteen buffalo, ten elk, ten mules, and a dozen other animals.[11]

The World's Columbian Exposition or Chicago World's Fair would celebrate the discovery of the New World by Christopher Columbus and would be the largest exposition of its kind. The Fair was an event so grandiose that it remains to this day the standard by which all other fairs are judged. Over 27,500,000 were in attendance.[12] Buffalo Bill's Wild West had been success at the American Exposition in London and at the Exposition Universelle in Paris. As far as Buffalo Bill and other organizers were concerned, the now-expanded Buffalo Bill's Wild West and Congress of Rough Riders of the World was on its way to Chicago. Buffalo Bill's request to be part of the Fair's midway was rejected by the committee. Soon Cody and his partners purchased fifteen acres opposite the fair's entrance. They paid a very high price, but it turned out to be one of their smartest business moves.[13] Many visitors who came to see the Fair attended Buffalo Bill's Wild West show and then left, more than satisfied. They thought the Wild West was the Fair![14]

Gurian horsemen. Reclining: Luka Chkhartishvili.

9. Coming to America

When the world's Columbian Exposition opened on May 1, 1893, Buffalo Bill's Wild West and Congress of Rough Riders of the World had already been working for one month. Rough Riders of the World came into their own as a major dimension of the show. American audience unfamiliar with gauchos, Arabians, and Cossacks saw them for the first time, performing feats of horsemanship. Cody was able to fill up his 18,000-seat arena almost every day. The season of 1893, from April through October, proved to be the Wild West's best. Between April 26 and October 12, more than five million people saw the Wild West, and the profits were in the millions of dollars.

For the most part, Georgian trick riders were short guys. "They are small, undersized, but wiry-looking men."[15] For instance, famed rider Luka Chkhartishvili's, height was five feet, two inches. As *Monday Morning* (July 27, 1896) stated, "Their leader is a swarthy little fellow, weighing not more than 140 pounds." Or, "Sitting comfortably on their high sad-

Sitting: **Kirile Khoperia.**

dles, the Cossacks looked wonderingly around. They were slight fellows for the most part. Ugly looking sabers hung at their sides and all of them had half-burned cigarettes."[16] It is not surprising, because for larger men to get used to the tricks performed by the Georgians would be difficult. But there were exceptions; the rider Kirile Khoperia, it is said, was almost two meters high, and he was considered as one of the finest trick riders among Georgians.

Georgian riders, most of whom had never traveled outside their native villages and never even been in their country's capital city, Tbilisi, were seriously impressed by the Western countries, especially by the United States. "I was tired out during the fifteen days of being in the ocean. Thanks God we went to New York City safely. Truly amazing city, you will never see anything better in your life," one horseman wrote in a letter to his family. "We are highly respected here; it is difficult to describe this respect. I'll just tell you that we have toilets made of marble stones. They look very expensive," wrote another.

According to Kirile Khoperia, they were living in "very tall buildings" and getting to their floor by tiny "moving rooms" (elevators). He mentioned the unusual clearness and order in the streets. Giorgi Chkhaidze wrote his family: "There are so many wires in the streets that birds often fly into them and fall down dead." Giorgi Chkhaidze would tell his relatives that Chicago streets were cleaned and buffed every single morning.

Almost in every town all over the world, curious crowds in the streets who wanted to have a closer look at their daggers and costumes often accosted the "Cossacks," although few dared approach them. People were literally mesmerized by the Georgians. "Vive Cosaques! Vive Cosaques!" is how admirers greeted the traditionally dressed and armed Georgian riders in the streets of Paris.[17] In 1905, according to another story, which surfaced in Paris, the riders were identified as Russian army deserters who refused to serve in Manchuria and came to France to enlist in the French Foreign Legion. This rumor caused an outbreak of idle talk in the French press. Some journalists even claimed that Russia did not have enough means to finance its army. On the face of it, the story was unconvincing, and soon the French public had to admit that the riders actually were not deserters but rather circus riders employed by the organizers of the Wild West show.

The daughter of Giorgi Chkhaidze, Ekaterine, remembers:

9. Coming to America

They started for America from Batumi, and it took them 21 days to reach Chicago. They lived in the countryside of Chicago surrounded by vast fields, where they used to train hard all day long. According to my father he was good at all kinds of tricks. He also visited France, England, Argentina, Mexico, and Italy. My father liked all foreign countries and people but not Englishmen. He used to say that they are very ambitious and arrogant people: "They liked our skills and were fascinated by our tricks but never expressed their admiration; it was different with other foreigners. In France we were always surrounded by people taking our photos. They called us Cossacks and we tried to explain that we were Georgians, but unfortunately they had no idea about Georgia. Our riders used to not sit but stand on the horses and showed eccentric and unique tricks, thus making the audience enraptured. In 1903 or 1904 they returned to Georgia having brought a lot of presents for our families and relatives. My father brought a zinc framed box that was kept in our family for a long time. According to my father there was a handsome guy among the Georgian riders that had wasted all his money on women and entertainment, and on his way home he had not a single dollar in his pocket. At that time a group of rich people were aboard our ship and this guy decided to give a performance to them. The Georgians started singing and he began dancing. This attracted a lot of people. The foreigners paid a lot to this guy and actually he made more money than his friends managed to save during their stay in America.

10. Promised Land

Buffalo Bill's show was an opportunity for poor peasants from Georgia to travel around the world, earn some money, and visit America. It was also an opportunity to meet fellow horsemen and share with them a thing or two. Luka Chkhartishvili, in one interview, stated, "We all love America. I do. It's a great country. I like the fact that there's lots of money here." A Georgian student with the pseudonym "Londoner" wrote in the *Tsnobis Purtsely*, "I've had several conversations with them and found out that they had been to every big city in the States. I also learned that they enjoyed the political order in the country, as well as its traditions and customs. They talk admiringly of the Americans' businesslike attitude, prosperity and bravery, although they also talk openly about people's impudence and undignified behavior in the big cities. Their favorite is California." "The climate, fruit and hospitality remind us of our home country," agreed the riders, "Some of the party has decided to stay in this country."[1]

"*Jesus, America is unbelievable!*" exclaims one rider in *Who's Guilty?*, a play (1908) by female playwright Nino Nakashidze. The play, extracts of which are below, was inspired by one trick rider's ill-fated story.

> Siko: *Say, Kharaman, is it true that the railroad goes underground in America and they have houses that reach to the skies?*
> Kharaman: *Sure, brother but that's nothing compared to other things. Even fairy tales don't have these things. Yeah, life happens there.*[2]

Some of the Georgians took up American residency and further claimed to spread democratic principles in their home country. Some American newspapers discovered that a number of Georgian Cossacks were known to have socialistic tendencies in their native land. One of the younger members, presumably Alexis Gogokhia-Georgian, said: "There are many of our people who have advanced ideas of liberty and are not in sympathy with the Russian government. I know of the socialistic labor party in this country. They have, however, somewhat different aims than the socialist of Russia. Many of our people are confident of a better government in time."³ Despite this, a number of American journalists tended to argue with the prevalent opinion, as expressed in *The Cleveland Plain Dealer*, which wrote on July 10, 1893, "While the reporter was in the tent Prince Dimitri Mgaloblishvili entered with his troop of royal Cossacks, twelve in number. These were attired in the exact costume represented on the show bill, with high riding boots tipped in the spurs, long Cossack cloaks and fur trimmed turbans. In their girdle they wore the regulation arms of their country. These Cossacks do some marvelous feats of horseback riding. This is the first time they have ever been out of their own country. They don't like America very well and are very homesick. An ironbound contract is the only thing which keeps them here."

The Georgian riders were filled with big hopes for the Western world as well as nostalgic feelings for their relatives and homeland. A museum in the Georgian city of Lanchkhuti has preserved some of their letters that highlight these emotions. Here are the extracts from the letters of Giorgi Gvarjaladze.

> My dearest Mishiko, I am asking the Almighty to have a chance to see you again. You are my soul, my dearest boy. Pelo [his wife], I am asking you to be wise and to take care of my child ... I was stupid to leave my dear boy, but now it is too late to talk about it... We rest for ten days and then we will start to work. The guys were very much happy when I joined them.... Do not sell Lomai [an ox]; do your best to buy another two cows.... Dear mother, please do your best to change a piece of roof of our house, don let it rot through....
>
> My dearest mother, I send you my greetings.... This year I have had a loss but what we can do ... this time I was making enough money just for my everyday expenses ... it is very difficult to work here. It is especially difficult to work in winter time in America. We are able to work at least two days a week to make a living ... I am very upset that this year was so hard for me, but still I am hopeful ... I would be able to make money in the future.⁴

An unknown rider wrote in his diary:

> It was on my twenty-ninth birthday. We had a small party; I invited not only Georgians, but locals as well. I bought several bottles of wine and prepared our national dishes: roasted piglet and chicken, "ghomi" [corn porridge] with Italian cheese. I even got our national spices.... The Americans licked their fingers ... Shalva was appointed as toastmaster. All of them could drink much. We talked, sang, had a wonderful time and parted very late. When I saw off my guests I looked up in the sky and it was full of stars. It reminded

Georgian Trick Riders in American Wild West Shows

Left to right: **Unidentified, cowgirl Goldie Griffith, Teophane Kavtaradze.**

me my childhood, when I was in Bakhmaro—I used to climb up a pear tree and look at the stars.

The pangs of homesickness never left the Georgian rider. "Christmas preparations were in full swing … I hewed chichilaki…. When my American friends saw it, they asked me to hew it for them too … nothing like that anyone had seen before. I did it … they were delighted."[5] A chichilaki is a Gurian-style Christmas tree made from straight hazelnut branches, shaved into the shape of a small coniferous tree, from 20 cm (8 in) to a few meters long.

Gradually, the number of riders' groups from Georgia increased. The *San Francisco Chronicle* (January 23, 1894) ran a long article called *Chief of the Steppes* about the "Russian nobleman" who "walked into the rotunda yesterday and finally strode up to the desk and registered, while a curious crowd looked on."

> No such a costume had ever been seen in the Palace before. The nobleman was six feet tall. He wore a long black garment, with a belt about the waist, and he had on his head a queer fez sort of a cap. Had it not been for some other features of his costume he would have been taken for a priest. These were a knife and a sword. The knife was a long one and hung from his belt, and the sword, which had a deep curve on it, looked like a cimeter.

10. Promised Land

After he had written his name in the language of the steppes he strode to the end of the room and sat down to wait for Russian Commissioner Hamburger and Assistant Commissioner Gelesnogrodoff. They did not come right away, and so he took out his sword and swashed the air with it a few times, while everybody stood from under. It was easy to see that the nobleman was in excellent health. He had the stride and the action generally of an athlete, and with his long and full black beard, dark eyes and really classic face he made a striking picture.

To those who have seen the famous Cossack rough riders of Buffalo Bill's show he seemed another such an intrepid spirit ... his name, as rendered in English, is M. T. Kotkoshvili [a Georgian name], and this the Assistant Commissioner afterward wrote on the register to supplement the curious characters which the native of Circassia had inscribed. The nobleman, when interviewed by aid of an interpreter, said he was from Tifliss, a town of some 50,000 people in the steppes.

Assistant Commissioner Gelesnogrodoff said, speaking of Kotkoshvili in detail:

He is the descendant of a noble Circassian family in Caucasus, and this town of Tifliss from which he comes has lately been so transformed, that now it has electric lights, nice buildings, a splendid theatre, telephones and all modern conveniences. The town is in the mountains and the country is like Switzerland.

"The Circassians are very fond of horses and are celebrated riders. The nobleman, Kotkoshvili, is one of the most clever of riders, and when he came to Chicago and met his countrymen who were engaged at Buffalo Bill's show he gave them special instructions in several of the most difficult performances. In doing this he was highly congratulated for perhaps only a few men live who possess the high art of riding Kotkoshvili does. He has lived literally on horseback, and the northern circus, as is well known, cannot begin to compass the feats done by the Cossack or Circassian riders."

"I have been riding the horses of my country," said the nobleman, "since I was 10 years old. The laws there require that all children, when they arrive at that age, shall spend most of their time in the saddle [in reality, there never was such a law]. This is why we have become a nation of good riders. Our horses, too, are, I think, the finest, with the greatest power of endurance of any in the world."

(The smaller version of this article was reprinted by Georgian newspaper *Iveria*, February 9, 1894). As it turned out, in 1894, the Society Circus had one Cossack rider, apparently Kotkoshvili.

Soon, many Georgian horsemen were systematically touring different countries. It is not an overstatement to say that the show's organizers had struck a gold mine—they had artists who attracted huge crowds. Since their arrival in America, they still roused huge interest from the media and the public. "Passing the small private tent of the colonel," wrote *The Herald* (July 28, 1897), "one of the cavalrymen, who acted as a guide, led the way into the large tent occupied by the Congress of Rough Riders."

> Here, sprawled about in the straw, lay the representatives of the nations, gathered, many of them, from the most removed quarters of the world by the agents of the Colonel for the entertainment of the American people. Each little party of strangers occupies a division of the large tent. Between the Bedouins and the South American Gauchos were the Cossacks. While the Gauchos were taking their after-supper siesta and the Arabs were engaged in preparing their elaborate toilets, our friends from Caucasia enjoyed their leisure in what a Yankee would call loafing. Georgian Tchaidze [he might be Giorgi Chkhaidze] was mending an old pair of boots. Alexis Evanovich [Alexis Gogokhia] was doing stunts with Peyotra Stephanovitch [unidentified] on the ropes outside for a wondering, gaping crowd of small boys. The Prince was smoking a real American cigarette.

Onophre Tsuladze.

More quotes from American sources, "There is very little information about why these people left their homes, but at least one group of Cossacks toured because they earned more money than they could at home and because they were needed for only six months."[6] One of the Georgian riders is of the same opinion in a letter written to his family, "We do make some pocket-money here but hopefully we are going to earn more in the future." Luka Chkhartishvili also stated, "I have father, mother, wife and children. They all live in Russia and I have to take some money for them in winter, if I don't break

10. Promised Land

my neck, of course."[7] Asked by a reporter what was his idea of having fun in his country, Luka responded, "Plenty of friends, plenty of wine, a good time."[8]

It must be said that not all of the riders went to America solely by preference. Some were fleeing punishment. A Gurian rider, Vaso Tsuladze, known by the name Sam Sergie (he performed in 1911–1914; reportedly he continued working in the Wild West shows after 1917) with his brother Onophre, also a future Wild West performer, fled to the States following a train robbery. It was said that during the robbery several people got killed. Later he used to show off a golden cigarette case engraved with a double-headed eagle, boasting that he took it from a Russian army officer. This is what had actually happened, according to Onophre's grandchild Otar Gvaberidze: some drunk Russian general and his fellows beat up several Lanchkhutians without any reason in Batumi. They heard this story in Lanchkhuti and discovered that the general was supposed to travel by that particular train. Vaso Tsuladze called on some people, and armed men stopped the train in Lesa, near the Lanchkhuti station. They entered the vans and started looking for the general. Soon Vaso found him, beat him up, and took away his golden cigarette case. Shortly Vaso went to the United States. After the 1917 Revolution he came back. When Soviet Russia annexed Independent Georgia in February 1921, Tsuladze fled to France. After couple of years he immigrated to America and in 1930 became a U.S. citizen. Soon he changed his name to Sam Sergie.

Vaso Tsuladze, circa 1913.

It is extremely interesting that Vaso Tsuladze was not the only Georgian rider who adopted the name Sam Sergie. There was another horseman with almost the same name Sergia. They were both from Lanchkhuti and were of the same age. There is no doubt that Sam Sergie and Vaso Tsuladze are one and the same person: pictures of Vaso from America and the signature on them confirms that Sergie is really Tsuladze. But uncertainty remains.

Here is the S.S. *Niagara*'s 1912 manifest, which provides interesting details of Vaso Tsuladze, Sam Sergia, and other Georgians:

Vaso Tsuladze, age twenty-eight, passage was paid by George, cash on hand $200, spent five years in the U.S., he lived at 119 South Morgan St. Chicago, was 5 ft 10 in tall, and was born in Lanchkhuti

Sam Sergia, age twenty-eight, passage was paid by Georgian, cash on hand $20, spent eight years in the U.S., he lived at 119 South Morgan St. Chicago, was 5 feet 7 in tall, was born in Lanchkhuti, and his wife's name was Christina.

Vaso Tsuladze, aka Sam Sergie, circa 1958.

George Georgian, age forty, paid for his own passage, cash on hand $500, spent eight years in the U.S.; he lived at 190 South Morgan St. Chicago, was 5 feet 6 in tall, had blue eyes and was born in Tbilisi.

Platon Murvanidze, age forty, passage was paid by Georgian, cash on hand $215, spent six years in the U.S., he lived at 119 South Morgan St. Chicago, was 5 feet 9 in tall, was born in Lanchkhuti, and his wife's name was Ephrasina Murvanidze.

Kaisar Kvitaishvili, age thirty, passage was paid by Georgian, cash on hand $25, spent nine years in the U.S., he lived at 119 South Morgan St. Chicago, was 5 feet 6 in tall, was born in Lanchkhuti, and his father's name was Petre Kvitaishvili.[9]

10. Promised Land

Sam Sergie was the owner of Stockman's Cafe in Fort Worth, Texas, for several years. In 1950 he had changed the name to the Stock Yards Recreation Club and in 1952 changed to Sam's Club. Sam Sergie died in Fort Worth in 1965 and was buried at the Mt. Olivet cemetery. Word has it that his lawyer took all his belongings after his death. Sam's Georgian friends in the United States protested but couldn't do anything at the time to stop the confiscation. Sam's brother Onophre returned to Georgia and died there.

In general, the Georgians' decision to travel to distant lands was based on financial hardship—touring meant profits. In the second half of the 19th century a great number of Gurians left their homes for work elsewhere. Between 1894 and 1905 the Gurian population decreased from 104,951 to 96,708.[10] It was a great chance for poor peasants to avoid hardship and economical and revolutionary shocks and earn good money. On occasion, group leaders were targeted with bribes in their native villages. For example, rider Tsetskhladze presented to Luka Chkhartishvili a white stallion, and only after the present, the latter took him to America. One rival wounded Jimshet Lomadze in the leg, but the wound was slight, so he could still go to the United States.

The American employers paid relatively good money, up to $40–50 per month. According to Frank Butler (husband of Annie Oakley), in the beginning of the Georgians' career, "We paid them the handsome salary of $1 a day."[11] The price of a cow in Georgia in those days was 3–5 rubles. In the *Tsnobis Purtsely* it was reported, "They are paid 100 rubles per month and are given a wonderful chance to see the world." Indeed, the money was good and the riders were paid two times a month,

Jimshet Lomadze with wife.

but only if they actually appeared in the shows. Securing themselves against unexpected departures, organizers paid the greater share of salaries at the end of the season. Giorgi Gvarjaladze wrote to his family,

> In case I will be employed by the shows I will be financially secure. Mother, I was thinking about sending you some money but I had to quit my job and couldn't find another one for a while. Now, thanks to Panteleimon Tsintsadze I'm engaged in a show again and hopefully will get $12 per week. It amounts to 25 rubles. If things go well they may pay us $13 per week. He has got a business for 15 dollars per week, but he has to keep some amount of money for his own benefit from that amount. Originally he wanted to hire somebody from Russia, but as there are so many of us unemployed he has changed his mind.... He offered to Laphier Mshvidobadze positions for three men ... and he offered four positions to Kaisar Chkonia. So Laphier Mshvidobadze, Iorama Mshvidobadze, Tsilosani and me ... all going to this place. Kaisar Chkonia, Kvitaishvili, Urushadze, and Nithipo are going to take the four men position.... The show has been performing for seven months this year ... working till November ... and will be opened from the first of April.... Panteleimon is 500 miles away from us now.... He stays where his show is now....

But not everybody would reach the "Promised Land" and accomplished American Dream. This extract is from a letter by Nikoloz Chkonia:

> We arrived in Neworg [sic; New York] on March 9 ... Kato, a very tragic incident happened to us. Meliton Tsintsadze fell ill in Odessa. The manager hired doctors and nurses who recommended leaving him there until he felt better, and then they promised they would send him to America to join us, but he didn't agree and asked us not to leave him there. We boarded the ship; the manager assigned a doctor and a nurse to him on board, but in vain. He asked us not to bury him at sea. He died at sea on March 4th. We took him to New York and then wanted to send his body to Georgia, but they asked for 2,000 rubles. Unfortunately none of us had enough money, so we had to bury him in New York. The funeral was exemplary. All the riders and all the horses were in black. We did all we could. Please go to Zurabi's, Data's families, inform Lukaia Ebralidze and other Lanchkhutians to have memorial service in his name....

The *New York Tribune* (March 20, 1898) published an article, apparently about the same event, "A Cossack Dies at Sea," which stated that a person named Alexander Tsintsadze, "one of the horde of Cossacks under contract to Buffalo Bill, died at sea from heart disease on the Campania on Tuesday afternoon, and the death caused great excite-

10. Promised Land

Dimitri Tsintsadze with Lanchkhutian ladies.

ment." Alexander Tsintsadze was forty years old and was born in Ozurgeti. "On his death the officers of the Campania ordered the body buried at sea as is usual, but his comrades entered a most vigorous protest, as they declared that in that case, upon their return to their native land, their countrymen would undoubtedly accuse them of the murder of the man. But they were told that they could get a death certificate signed by the Consul-General which they could show to their countrymen. They demanded that the body be brought to port and buried ashore. Their request was finally acceded to by the officers." He was buried at the Green-Wood Cemetery in Brooklyn, New York, under the name of Alexander Tsintsadze.

I discovered that a lot of the Georgian or American records are incorrect, and Meliton Tsintsadze's case is one of them. First of all, I couldn't connect the author of the letter, Nikoloz Chkonia, with any "Cossack" group at this period. In spite of this I have the rider with such name in my "Riders' list." Secondly, there is no records of Meliton

Tsintsadze coming to America; he was only in Buffalo Bill's Wild West 1892 London show. So far, Meliton-Alexander Tsintsadze's puzzle remains unsolved.

Despite their hardships, the riders somehow managed to send money to their relatives. The "Londoner" commented on this tradition admiringly.

> After the show I found those Gurians. They were surprised and very happy to see a Georgian in a foreign country. They flooded me with questions. We talked for a long time. I gave them the Georgian newspapers and sent them articles from time to time. It's amazing, but one rider asked me to get him the London university program for his brother; apparently he was financially supporting his studies. The other one told me that he did the same for his relative who was studying medicine. I looked at these Gurians and could hardly stay on foot because of great joy. They didn't speak Russian (except Kadjaia, who is their head and speaks fluent Russian). They were not educated at all but were eager to help their family members to get education. Due to this they used to send them money. It points to the wise nature that is the basis of the future development, and also underlines the fact they are offsprings of well-educated and noble ancestors.

A reporter for the *New York Dramatic Mirror* happened to visit the office of Edwin H. Low in New York and saw four "Cossacks" there. When the reporter asked about the visitors, Low replied, "I am transporting these persons from Chicago to a remote place in Russia. They are part of a band of Cossacks that I brought to this country under contract with Forepaugh's circus. The main part of the troupe still remains in this country, but these four, for some reason that I do not fully understand, are recalled. I am required to see that they get back."[12] At times, due to the financial problems the Wild West show, managers needed to reduce the number of performers in their shows or circuses. Soon the four Georgian "Cossacks" were boarded onto the ship and on their way home.

Money shortages often forced the riders to look for side jobs. Luka Chkartishvili would send secondhand clothes to Guria for sale; Panteleimon Tsintsadze, for example, had to take a job at a large company. Superficially, everything went well. He married his employer's daughter and immigrated to America, but after a while his nostalgia for his homeland grew, and although he wanted to return, he could not because Georgia was already overtaken by the Soviets.

10. Promised Land

On one occasion, the Georgian riders went on strike against Buffalo Bill Cody and "Cossack" leader David Kadjaia in Paris. The horsemen demanded a raise in salary. According to *The New York Times* (May 14, 1905), "Cody is having trouble with his Cossacks, 14 of whom demanded a rise in salary this week, considering the extra expense of living in Paris. Meeting a refusal, they struck and left the show. The Colonel promptly instituted a lawsuit, asking for 500f [$100] damage each." Those riders were: Solomon Imnadze, Silovan Chkhartishvili, Pavle Makharadze, Simon Oragvelidze, Nikoloz Tsintsadze, Khariton Chkonia, Miron Chkonia, Ivane Baramidze, Ivane Jorbenadze, Nikoloz Surguladze, and Ushangi Kvitaishvili. *The New York Times* wrote, "The strike leaders threatened those of their comrades who hesitated to join them, declaring that their homes would be burned and their families massacred after their return to Russia."[13] After three days, the riders asked Cody to take them back, but it was too late, and other riders had replaced them. However, later it seems that some of them were admitted back into the show, because their names appear again on the Wild West programs. The *New York Clipper* described another incident. "A band of Cossacks who have been touring with the Forepaugh circus last week entered a bill for two-thousand dollars, claiming a breach of contract. The matter was satisfactorily settled."[14] The Georgians, it appeared, were not paid during May.

Joseph Mshvidobadze.

Some of the riders had to take rough with the smooth, and the story of Joseph Mshvidobadze is a good example. He was invited to join a group of riders in the United States by his friend Dimitri Tsintsadze. The tragic news that an epidemic disease had taken the lives of his wife and five of his children reached him somewhere in the Midwest. His first reaction was to leave everything behind and settle in America, but later he made the decision to go back to Georgia for the sake of his two remaining elder sons. He did so and invested nearly all his savings in a shop for Kvirosi, his eldest son. When the shop was ready, he sent Kvirosi to Batumi to buy some goods. One day, when Joseph was returning from the field, he was captured by robbers who asked for all his savings. Joseph had no money at the time and was killed. Beside himself with grief, Kvirosi sold the shop, bought a rifle, revolvers, and ammunition, and set out to follow his father's killers in order to settle the score. He couldn't find them. Well-wishers suggested that he should pass the task on to professional killers. He agreed and found two men who promised to do the job but refused to take money out of respect for his father: "Your father was a great man, and for his memory we will find them all." The job was accomplished in the shortest time possible, and five men were killed within a month, two of them on the place where Joseph was murdered. Only one out of five managed to escape from the revenge, but when, after twenty years in hiding, he came back to Georgia, he was also killed in the yard of Joseph's house.

11. All Born Princes: Daredevils

As a rule, all Georgian riders had to enter into a contract to participate in the shows. Circuses and Wild West shows had a pay system that included a hold-back of the first two weeks of pay. This assured the employees continued employment during the season.

Here's the Cossack pay list: Noe Tsilosani, Ivane Baramidze, Khariton Chkonia, Miron Chkonia, Alexander Murvanidze, Islam Urushadze, Vaso Tsuladze. Pay for the week of April 30, 1910, was $7.50—One Week hold back (savings at the end of season). Pay for the week of May 7 was $10. Rate = $10 per week.

The performers were only paid for actual performance days. For example, for a rained-out show, or for any other reason the performance failed, the managers deducted a day's pay. An injured artist who could not perform or who missed a show did not get paid. Some Wild West show programs assured the general public that hurt performers were taken care of by the show. However, this only applied to accidents outside their acts, such as train wrecks or other natural disasters. A performer hurt in the arena was liable for his or her own injuries.[1]

Usually when show was closed, riders went home. "He [Prince Luka] goes home each year when the season ends, and is sent here again by Mr. Kean, the foreign agent who sent over the Cossack riders."[2] Those riders who wanted to stay in the United States had to take care of themselves. The Georgian riders worked under this pay system during all their Wild West and circus careers.

According the contract's strict terms and code of behavior, the riders had to keep their costumes and weapons clean and tidy, act like gentlemen, and avoid drinking alcoholic beverages and gambling, fistfights, and sleeping in their riding boots. "There were some silly rules in the show like forbidding one to go to bed in his boots. Have you ever heard of such nonsense? Maybe I am an uneducated man, but it does not mean that I am stupid! It was also prohibited to talk to women from the arena, but later on they stuck to our guys like ticks ..." wrote an unknown rider. There were limitations on luggage as well and a strict prohibition on

Kvirosi Mshvidobadze.

domestic animals. Only Indians were allowed to have dogs, as they were part of a show.

For the sake of fairness it must be noted that the Georgians tried their best to behave well. According to a newspaper, "They have not the trappings of princes, but they have the lordly manners and the conscious dignity, which is said to be the surest sign of what is known as high breeding. If you are to believe them they are 'all born princes.'"[3] Here's an extract from William E. Curtis's book regarding the title of Prince.

> It's a joke among the Russians that every Georgian is a nobleman and that your porter or drosky [horse-drawn carriage] driver is certain to be a baron or perhaps a count. It is undoubtedly true that titles were once bestowed with lavish generosity by the Georgian kings, who paid their debts as well as rewarded merit by conferring rank promiscuously. A gentleman remarked the other day, however, that the only title worth taking off your hat to is that of a prince. Every large landowner is a prince. I do not know that it is necessary for him to have any given area. As a rule, a Georgian nobleman looks and dresses the part much more naturally than Russian or other European dukes and princes.[4]

In those days Russians commented on the number of Georgian princes, saying that every man owning one hundred sheep was a prince in Georgia. Once one Russian asked a Georgian if this story was true. "No, I don't think so," he replied, "because I know a Georgian who has about 200 million sheep and he is not a prince." He meant Joseph Stalin.[5]

The *Brooklyn Sunday Citizen* (May 20, 1894) provides a description of the show's participants' tent and among them, the Georgians':

> The Cossacks have a square wall tent, which they keep in excellent condition, whether the occupant be a prince or peasant, and only the two classes are represented. There are two princes in the troupe. According to the best phonetic rendering of their names as spoken—spelling them out was precluded by the difference in the Russian and Latin letters—they are Prince Loucca Tchkartichville [Chkhartishvili] and Prince Cio [Shio] Nakaidze. The latter is the wearer of two medals conferred upon him by Alexander III of Russia for services in the Russo-Turkish war. These princes are hereditary land owners in the Caucasus, their estates being now, since serfdom is abolished, let out in small holdings on tithe-rent, which is collected in kind of the crop or vintage. The title of prince is not quite so high in Russia as in most European countries, being equivalent, perhaps, to the German baron or the Italian count. Prince Loucca is, however, a man of wealth, and joined the rough riders a largely to gain knowledge of the western world.

As devoted Christians, the Georgians attended service, usually at the Catholic or Greek Church. Most of the riders were of the Russian Orthodox Church, which resembles the Greek Church. A few, however, were Roman Catholics, and among them Frida Mgaloblishvili. As a rule,

Markoz Jgenti.

11. All Born Princes

before departure Georgians presented the Georgian Church with charitable contributions. Jimshet Lomadze and Bartlome Kiladze presented the Church of Jacob the Apostle with a big wall candlestick and two smaller table candlesticks for their safe return to the village Mamati.[6]

One reporter described a Cossack who was ready to have a good time in town: "And that Cossack, what's he putting on his pink frock coat for and curling his mustache before the mirror for, as if he was going on to do the Merry Widow act, when there isn't a show for twenty-four hours? Where's a fellow to get the delightful disillusionment of 'behind?'"

A showman responded: "Well," said the unruffled showman, "it happens that that Cossack is human and thinks his own costume the correct one like everybody else does. He's probably on his way down town to catch the eyes of the Kansas City maidens and whisper in their ears, if he can get close enough, that all real gentlemen wear pink frock coats."[7]

Based on the words of Kirile Khoperia and Giorgi Chkaidze, they usually visited the restaurants dressed in their best and always kept an eye on each other in case they didn't know how to handle an unknown dish. One reporter described the Wild West show camp "to see how Buffalo Bill gets up meals for his little polyglot family of five hundred and ten people."

Open-air housekeeping is the order of the day at the kitchen department of Col-

Kirile Khoperia.

onel Cody's tepee, and the appetites of Cossacks, scouts, cowboys, Bedouins, Mexicans, grooms, canvasmen, Indians, side-show freaks, soldiers and all other attaches of the big "Congress of Rough Riders" center about a single wagon which stands between the Coliseum Building and the tracks of the Illinois Central Railroad [Gurians stayed in the coliseum's upper balcony gallery, with their laundry of colored clothes drying on the balcony seats and railing]. This one wagon is the gastronomic hub around which revolve half a thousand hungry digestions—and they make the circuit three times every day, rain or shine, without regard to the box-office receipts and with the persistent regularity of the sun. Consequently the "range wagon" is almost as important a piece of impedimenta to this big band of pilgrims as was the ark to the ancient Israelites.[8]

The locals used to comment on Cossacks' appetite, saying that they could easily digest stones.

The Russian Cossacks eat very much like they ride—at a gallop and without regard to the laws of health. Mastication cuts no ice with them; they could apparently digest rocks if necessary, after having swallowed them whole.[9]

The chief cook of Buffalo Bill stated in one of his interviews,

We prepare 800 to 1000 individual steaks every morning and serve them for breakfast. They are all done on this single range, over five griddle holes inside of twenty-five minutes by the watch. Oh, the boys love the steaks! The Cossacks and the Indians want 'em three times a day—and they get 'em, too! We have to suit all sorts of tastes here, the same as at a fashionable hotel.[10]

Every day fifteen cooks and forty waiters served the meal. Breakfast usually consisted of cereals, beefsteak, bacon and eggs, pork chops, griddle cakes, lamb chops, fish cakes, hot biscuit or rolls, tea, coffee, and milk. Dinner consisted of corned beef hash, pork and ham, beef and ham, beef stew or kidney pie, hamburger roast, cold roast beef, doughnuts, and dessert with tea, coffee, and milk. And supper: vegetable soup, roasts of beef, mutton and ham, boiled or mashed potatoes, other vegetables, and dessert. To supply the shows' huge cast there were required 600 lbs of beef, 350 lbs of pork, 500 lbs of mutton and lamb, 120 lbs of coffee, 400 gallons of milk, 800 loaves of bread, and from 250 to 350 lbs of sugar. There must be on hand daily six bushels of carrots, thirty bushels of potatoes, 22 bushels of turnips, 12 doz. cans of tomatoes, and a like number of corn or succotash, besides supplies of vegetables in like quantity.[11]

11. All Born Princes

Georgian horsemen with unknown American.

For Georgian riders, such a variety of food was uncommon. The Gurian kitchen is dominated by vegetables: pkhali (spinach) and walnut salad, beans prepared with unique local seasoning, eggplants with walnuts and spices, ghomi (corn porridge), mchadi (corn bread), satsivi (sauce made of walnuts and served cold), also khachapuri (cheese-filled bread), fish, roasted or boiled chicken, or turkey with sauce, and other.

The *Lincoln State Journal* noted: "The Russian Cossacks go it strong for a goulash and prefer meat stews to roasts or even poultry. They are great coffee drinkers and will get away with half dozen cups at a meal. Not one of the Cossacks with the show used either milk or sugar in coffee."[12] One time, the Georgians, not conversant in English, entered a canteen and asked for scrambled eggs. The waiter didn't understand until Serapion Imnadze crouched and doodled around the place like a hen. They had scrambled eggs that day.

Sarah J. Blackstone wrote, "The Wild West horses took a while to become accustomed to such strange riding habits as a Cossack riding backwards or standing on his head in the saddle."[13] Some Georgian and foreign sources claim, rather unconvincingly, that they rode the Georgian breeds. They rode American ponies. According to the *London Start* (May 31, 1892), "Their riding consists mainly of tricks on horseback, and I'm very anxious to see what they can do in that line. We cannot try them yet, as their wiry little horses need rest after their long journey." But these comments don't correspond to reality. First, it was very expensive (around $320 to transport only a rider across the Atlantic), and second, it was prohibited by quarantine regulations. Another citation from Nino Nakashidze's play confirms this point:

> Kharaman: *I don't know about others but those who come to us make loads of money. Trips take nothing, living there is cheap. Horses are provided. All you have to do is ride and be happy. Then, you grab your money and do whatever you wish with it. Wanna send it to relatives? OK, wanna have fun? Fine.*[14]

When asked about it, Ivane Makharadze said: "Our horses? They couldn't have borne the journey. We ourselves had difficulties in crossing the Black Sea, let alone our horses. But we brought our saddles, our whips, and the rest of the stuff."[15] Here's an interesting bit from another American newspaper,

Serapion Imnadze.

11. All Born Princes

The Cossack saddle is another thing that attracts much attention. Its chief peculiarity, seen from the sides, is two thin pads, fore and after, resembling loaves of bread. A closer examination shows there are four of these pads. The Cossack stands up in the stirrups with two or three pads on, before and behind his legs. They are stuffed with horsehair. "Why does the Cossack use this saddle?" Prince Luka, a Georgian Cossack, could only shrug his shoulders when the question was asked him. All he could state positively was that style of saddle had been used in his native section of the Caucasus as long as human memory could extend.[16]

Indianapolis News (May 21, 1901) reported on the saddles:

> The Cossacks were commented on freely, for it is generally understood by the public that their milk of human kindness has turned sour, and their high saddles seem a never-ending source of interest, though, as one man remarked in the crowd: "If they want camels, why don't they get them, and not try to make a camel out of a horse." The "Cossacks" have a small horn at both ends of their saddles. While doing vaults of any kind, one hand is held on the horn and the other holds a leather thong tied at the base of the horn.[17]

But there were exceptions: Luka Chkhartishvili was standing on the galloping horse (sometimes on the bare horse) without any thongs or any help, as seen in some photos. These saddles were not cheap; an ordinary Cossack saddle cost $75, and the one custom made, which had padding about six inches thick stuffed with deer hair and with ivory mountings, for Alexis Georgian cost $275. Once Luka Chkhartishvili was interested in a hunting saddle, "but didn't think much of it compared with his own.... It was all right for 'parade' riding, but no good to lie back in or stand on your head on."[18] Reporters also were surprised by their stirrups, which were very small, only big enough to get the points of the toes into, and drawn short.

> A man must be a good rider who can occupy that aerial roost and steady himself by those toy stirrups. Their feats set one to guessing what they do them for. Do they twine themselves all over their horses because it is hard to do, or has it all some warlike purpose? The most of it looks as if it were just the dare-devil nature of the men, but such perfection of the management of a horse, and of one's self in the saddle, must be useful to a fighting man, too.[19]

"Cossack" saddles can be seen today at the Tom Mix Museum in Dewey, Oklahoma, the Buffalo Bill Center of the West, Cody, Wyoming, and the Cowboy Hall of Fame in Oklahoma City.

Sergi Gvarjaladze.

To feed, lodge, and generally maintain a body of 800 men of mixed nationalities and, furthermore, to exhibit them before the public twice a day in special performances constitutes a task of some magnitude. But when, in addition, matters are so admirably arranged that the whole of them, together with the entire equipment of the show, which includes about 600 horses and

11. All Born Princes

numberless weapons, can migrate from one town to another in a single night, it becomes a most remarkable feat. They carried a canvas arena in which could be seated 20,000 people, and which was used when a building cannot be found in a town large enough for a show.

The exhibition in the open air had a seating capacity for 12,000 people. The seats are covered with waterproof canvass sheds, perfect protection against sun and rain, and the performance is given, whether it is clear, cloudy, raining or snowing.[20]

Buffalo Bill's crew built, performed in, dismantled, transported, and rebuilt their arena in 24 hours, week after week, on their summer tours. Canvas stables for 600 horses are also carried, in addition to a dining tent, in which meals for 800 people engaged in the show are served three times a day. It is said everything worked as smoothly as if Buffalo Bill's Wild West was only a small theatrical company.[21]

The "Wild West" show comes from the East, where it has just finished a very successful season. The outfit is almost new, 200 new horses having been added to the large number already on hand to take the place of these killed

Nestor Menagarishvili.

in the railroad accident that befell the show last fall. Forty of these animals are known as the "outlaw" bronchos, which startled the New Yorkers with their wild antics for a long season. Broncho "busting," a vivid illustration of cowboy life in our cattle States, will be seen at every exhibition. The Indian with his war whoop and paint will be there, and a corps of United States Atlantic coast guards will give a very interesting exhibition of their occupation of rescuing people from the sea. One of the biggest features to the exhibition will be a military spectacle of the battle of San Juan Hill, Cuba, which will be put on with the assistance of actual participants. Frontier battles between the white and the red men will be depicted, true to the thrilling scenes of early life on the plains.

This will be the last visit of Buffalo Bill (Colonel Cody) to this coast for some time, as he intends taking his performance to Europe for several years. Two performances will be given daily, at 2 and 8 p.m. rain or shine. The performance will be given in open air, but the spectators will be protected from the elements by huge canvas covers.[22]

At times the performance was plagued by bad weather, which put to the test the show's promise to perform come rain or shine. Some days the rain was so heavy that it was only with difficulty that the performers were seen at times. The arena was rain-soaked, with mud a foot deep.

The great wagons were thoroughly embalmed up to the body in the mud and it looked like an impossible task to free them. After six and eight horses had been hitched on and made an inglorious failure, after the number had been doubled and tripled without success, the show looked more deeply foundered than was at first sensed. The horses floundered and went down, their own weight burying them well-nigh out of sight. In helping them out, the old process of holding a horse's head down was abandoned and his head was raised instead. All night the work went on in the rain, and word was finally taken to Col. Cody that the show was anchored for twenty-four hours probably. The mud seemed to get more and more without bottom and in the midst of it all one of the biggest wagons went over on its side and landed in a position that offered a wonderful field for work. Every rope in the show was brought into use and every man, irrespective of nationality, lined up for the tug of war. After much labor, victory crowned the efforts and the vehicle was raised. At daybreak no change was instituted in the proceedings and one by one the heavy wagons were raised and drawn to the road. As many as thirty-four horses had to be used in some cases and then the work was accomplished only with great difficulty. The only clean place was the top of the rail cars, where representatives of a dozen different nations sat. The Indians strutted around in full war paint, more or less streaked with the rain and fire water, and punched the Cuban insurgents in the ribs. The dark

11. All Born Princes

visage Cossack smoked cigarettes and chewed peanuts, while the young Arabs spent the day trying to hit the telegraph wires with stones.[23]

In bad weather the rehearsals and performances were conducted on muddy grounds. Once during the performance, "one of the Cossack rider's horses fell on the slippery track when his rider was in the act of picking a handkerchief from the ground at full gallop, but horse and rider appeared to have a mutual understanding on the subject and rolled in opposite directions, getting up to have another try at the handkerchief, which was captured without trouble."[24]

The usual performance of Georgians began with the riders, all dressed in national outfits (chokha), taking the stage while carrying their weapons and singing. Gurians rarely dressed in Gurian outfits—kabalakhi, male headwear or highly ornate fabric; the neck line was always cut high, and chakura—a kind of chokha, a man's outer, short coat.

The unknown rider, while he worked in the post office, in his diary recalled the first time he saw a Wild West show and the Georgian riders: "The Indians appeared, they shouted and robbed and killed the farmers. Soon cavalry appeared, they fired guns and screamed, they killed all Indians and released white farmers. Everybody was satisfied. Then announced the exit of the Cossacks, I thought they probably came from Russia.... Twelve riders made one lap and suddenly began to sing the Georgian song. From surprise I even jumped, they are my compatriots, I said...."

First Georgian riders with drawn swords swept round the arena two or three times at full speed. At a given signal they suddenly stopped and dismounted on mid-stage, broke into a new song, and started to perform one of Georgian native dances to the accompaniment of handclaps. Sometimes this dance was executed upon a wooden platform. The unidentified newspaper (June, 1892) reported: "The performances were primarily the Cossacks, who look at first sight rather like Persian horse dealers, with their head-dresses cut down; and, indeed, they have a distinctly Oriental character about them all through. They ride in singing a song, the like of which may be heard on any evening in an East Indian bazaar. Then three of them dismount and dance, but their dance is more suggestive of Limerick than Lucknow, being the very image of an Irish jig."

The emotional Georgian native dance was a new fruit for the "civilized" audience. As one reporter put it, it was just "skipping about in an idiotic manner." But there were some who gave the Georgian dance its due. "They dance over swords in a light-footed and crazy way," wrote Frederic Remington.[25]

> Though they are men of war, they will trip the light fantastic toe with the best, and they can dance as lightly as a ballerina." [This extract is from an old, unidentified English-language newspaper, the remains of which are preserved in rider Pavle Makharadze's family house]. "The last novelty introduced at the latter entertainment comprises a company of Cossacks, whose evolutions render a second visit a necessity. Their dismounting is a marvel of rapid execution, and their terpsichorean performances, for they do dance in spite of their long costumes, are equally astonishing. The movements of the men are electric, and their very legs are provocative of sentiment; now compelling your admiration by whirl and poise: now, by rapid inversion of knees and toes, producing an indescribable grotesqueness. Their feats of horsemanship are amazing for pace and skill. One member of the troupe flies along sitting astride in reversed position, another rides upon his shoulder, and a third upon his head; these topsy-turvy adventures called forth a storm of plaudits; and the leader, not to be outdone, makes the circuit of the arena, alighting and remounting a dozen times while his horse is at full gallop.[26]

The Wild West program didn't change much over the years. Georgians rode in the arena five times in each show. They first rode in the Grand Entree, and their second entry was a race between Cossacks, Indians, cowboys, and Mexicans. Their third event was to give a ten-minute performance of native song, dance, and riding. Before the end of the show, they took part in the hippodrome races and the final salute. The total time in the arena was approximately fifteen minutes twice a day and participation in the daily parade. Their stunt riding represented the perfection of man and horse, and the Georgians did the most unbelievable stunts while galloping. According to the unknown rider, "We used to impress the audience with our tricks while galloping. I used to pick up different things from the ground and perform somersaults; it was so exciting for the audience that even in awful weather it was impossible to find an empty seat."

The riders performed a series of maneuvers: at full gallop they were standing on their heads, standing straight in the saddle, swinging themselves parallel with their horses' sides, riding three or four horses simultaneously, diving under their horses' sides, jumping to the ground and then back, riding backwards, picking up stones, whips, handkerchiefs,

11. All Born Princes

hats, rifles, and other objects from the ground. They did "Possum Belly" rides while one rider played a concertina and another did vaults with his head and body enclosed in a sack tied around the waist. Some of the tricks were very popular with the spectators, such as the rider at full gallop standing on horseback and shooting. Also very admired was the game "Hold the Handkerchief," when riders were pursuing the one who was holding the handkerchief in his teeth and trying to take it away.

> The dancing and singing of the terra cotta coated riders was as unique as their horseback exhibition, and their part of the day's programme concluded with a running fight for a pocket handkerchief, which the princess and the stalwart Sgt. Andre Kcincatzi [Alexander Tsintsadze] succeeded in carrying off from the rest of the rough riders in a break-neck race around the hippodrome track.[27]

According to Frank E. Dean, Georgian riders probably have the distinction of originating the largest mass riding stunt done on one horse. They call this "The Feast Table Ride." Four men ride on one horse. One is backward on the neck, two others stand in the stirrups on each side waving bottles and holding a square board or table top between them, and the fourth rides sitting forward behind the saddle! The two stirrup riders each have a leg extended across the saddle for the opposite rider to sit astride, thereby "locking" them in place and enabling them to ride free-handed.[28]

Georgian riders, circa 1902 (courtesy Denver Public Library).

The Cossacks' riding takes your breath away. In spurred boots and long coats they stand on their horses' backs, lashing them furiously and inciting them to a madder speed with piercing cries, riding without check or rein. They sway far over and back, lean out, and bending low with a swift motion catch an object and wave it wildly as they swing their bodies up again to the saddle. It looks like a delirium of riding.[29]

Georgians performed some risky tricks, carried out by only a chosen few. In one of these tricks, a rider removed his saddle and dismounted while riding at a full gallop and then remounted again, fixing the saddle back onto the horse. This trick wasn't documented, but it is said that it was carried out by female rider Maro Zakareishvili.

The author Frank E. Dean wrote:

The Russian Cossacks specialized in drags and when they dreamed this one up they definitely threw precaution to the winds. Picture the Cossack blithely off the air to dangle by one foot against the shoulders of his horse. Remember that he did this in the full military dress of the Czar—and often included a long saber clenched in the teeth.

The American trick rider does the same trick but, having a practical turn of mind, leaves to the Cossack the special joy of impaling himself on his saber.[30]

This trick riding style is called dzhigitovka—a Turkic word taken to mean a skillful and courageous rider. It's one of the original national sports found among the people of Central Asia, Kazakhstan, and Caucasus. Participants must have high dexterity and skillful and courageous horse management.

The history of trick riding goes back to the fellow who climbed on his horse in the conventional manner and decided it would be faster to make a running jump. A groom in the stables of Rome experimented with the idea of standing on a running horse and, by the fourth century, Romans were howling in the Circus Maximus at the horse races in which the riders rode standing up. Later the armies of the world taught basic trick riding so that men would be better able to take care of themselves on horseback. The soldiers were taught to vault to their saddles, to pick up objects from the ground, perhaps a sword or a wounded comrade, and to do a "Hidden Ride." This last named feat was a good deal similar to the present-day rodeo trick riders' "Fender Drag" and enabled the rider to provide a smaller, if not invisible, target for the enemy marksman.[31] In the end of his book, Frank E. Dean provides the list of professional

11. All Born Princes

Unknown trick rider (courtesy Buffalo Bill Museum and Grave, Golden, Colorado).

trick riders, including the "Cossacks": Tephon-Teophane Kavtaradze, Ishlah-?, Prince Welikow-Veliko Kvitaishvili, Emily Welikow-Barbale Imnadze, Prince Luke-Luka Chkhartishvili, Captain Giorgi-George Georgian (or Alexis Georgian).

Georgian Trick Riders in American Wild West Shows

The Philadelphia Inquirer (April 18, 1893) wrote:

The much discussed Cossacks were disappointing in an agreeable sense; much has been expected of them and they surpassed by far everything that had been expected. They are truly the greatest riders in the world. Their performances almost surpass belief. They seem to defy every law of gravitation and to be simply inseparable from their horses. They cling to them as a needle does to a magnet, no matter what position they may assume. Riding backwards, standing in their saddles and picking coins from the ground and similar feats are done while their horses are galloping about the race course and this is done with astounding ease, grace and dexterity. They were frequently cheered and made a most emphatic hit.

According to the "Londoner," one British fan exclaimed,

"They are amazing! I've been to many places and got to know lots of riders in America and Australia, but I've never seen anything like that before. What I'm struck by most is that they seem to grow out of their horses. You can't even tell where the man ends and where the horse starts. The riding school they are from must be perfect. Amazing! Well, the Mexicans we have just seen can ride, of course, but they don't have the same kinetic stage presence. You are right, no school can provide the same skills. They must have it in their blood." I answered. "You are mistaken; there are no special schools for riders in Georgia. These are ordinary village youth. In their village they are used to demonstrating their riding skills in front of village girls and brides."

More quotes from American newspapers testify to their unique riding skill. "They stood in the saddle, on their feet and on their hands and kicked their legs as the horses flew madly around. They rode standing in their saddles with their faces facing their horses' tails and chased each other to capture a handkerchief carried in their mouth."[32]

"The strangely garbed Cossacks from the far off Caucasus mountains, the most expert riders in all Europe, perform feats of daring horsemanship that make even our reckless cowboys take notice and admire them."[33]

"The savage Cossacks did the greatest riding at last night's exhibition. The most thrilling riding was done by the Cossacks, standing on their high saddles and riding at breakneck speed, or dashing away with one heel on the saddle and head within an inch of the ground."[34]

When it comes down to sheer reckless riding, those wonderful rough riders of the Czar's cavalry have the world beaten. They tore about the enclosure yesterday in a way that chased the thrills up and down several thousand spines in the grandstand. With one foot in the stirrup and hinging backward

11. All Born Princes

till his body almost trailed along the ground, each Cossack urged his horse at full gallop around the arena. Standing up in the saddle is child's play to them. They all rode like mad yesterday standing on their heads on the horses' backs.[35]

"If the audience will watch Prince Lucca, the Cossack, with his sword, while standing on his saddle, they will be amazed, for so expert is he that as Remington, the famous artist, expressed it, 'No Cossack could commit suicide unless on the ground.'"[36]

"Our cowboys are universally the best exponents of expert horsemanship, but the famous Cossacks are their close rival."[37]

> Equestrianism in all its reckless and skillful forms was displayed in the arena of the show. Every performer—cowboy, cowgirl, or Indian—was a product of the prairie, except the contingent of Cossacks, under the leadership of Prince Lucca.... The Cossacks did not attempt the bronco riding feats of the cowboys, but they performed acrobatic exploits that for sheer, dare-devil achievement were sensational.[38]

In general, public and media called them acrobats rather than superior horsemen. Buffalo Bill Cody once said: "The Cossacks are marvelous horsemen, and do more fancy acrobatic feats than any other class of riders, but show me the Cossack who can ride a bucking bronco."[39] In reply to Cody, female rider Frida Mgaloblishvili supported the Georgian riding technique and claimed that the Cossacks were the best. "I have seen Buffalo Bill in Paris and in England," she said, "and the American, what you call Cowboy, they ride well, but you give our Cossack a bucking horse and he can sit him as well as the cowboy, even better, and he can do also many other things which the cowboy, he does not do."[40]

There was debate about who was considered as the best rider. As one group after another raced about the arena, the audience was urged to take sides and declare its choice. It did so with shout and cheers. For showman Johnny Baker there was no question that the gauchos were the finest of all riders. Others, mostly Americans, preferred cowboys. Pawnee Bill always supported the American cowboy—"the perfect embodiment of natural chivalry." A program from the show describes cowboys as the most daring, most skillful, most graceful, and most useful horsemen in the world. They fulfill the metaphor of the fabled centaur, believed to have been a demi-god, half horse, half man, only that the cowboy excels the centaur in being "an independent man who controlled the best points of the quadruped and made 'man's best friend' subservient to his needs, his pleasures and his pastimes.... Without the cowboy, civilization would have been hemmed in, and the fair States and Territories of the glorious West would have remained a howling wilderness to date."[41] Americans compared their frontier horsemen, Indians, and cowboys to legendary, exotic riding contingents from the Old World, including Cossacks, Gypsies, and Turkmen. Cossacks were hard, rough riders, and theirs was a contest to prove that in horsemanship the cowboys would come out second best.[42] Frederic Remington, whose artist's eye was delighted by the Cossacks, in 1892 wrote from London:

> The Cossacks will charge you with drawn sabers in a most genuine way, will hover over you like buzzards on a battlefield. They soar and whirl about in graceful curves, giving an uncanny impression, which has doubtless been felt by many a poor Russian soldier from the wheat fields of Central Europe as he lay with a bullet in him on some distant field. They march slowly around over imaginary steppes, singing in a most dolorous way, looking as they did in Joseph Brandt's paintings. They dance over swords in a light-footed and crazy way, and do feats on their running horses, which bring the handclapping. They stand on their heads, vault on and off, chase each other in a game called chasing the handkerchief, and they reach down at top speed and mark the ground with a stick. Their long coat tails flap out behind like an animated rag bag, while their legs and arms are visible by turns. Their grip on the horse is maintained by a clever use of these stirrups, which are twisted and crossed at will. They are armed like "pincushions," and ride on a big leather bag which makes their seat abnormally high.[43]

When Theodore Roosevelt was running for governor of New York, he was using his Rough Rider San Juan Hill charge in his campaign. *The Brooklyn Daily Eagle* (October 23, 1898) asked the question: "Does Theodore Roosevelt expect to carry this state on his merits as a Rough Rider? If so, why did the Republican Party not nominate a Russian Cossack as their candidate? I am sure a Cossack is much rougher in his riding than Theodore Roosevelt." The Georgians unintentionally got entangled in American politics, but the Americans admitted (once again) that Cossacks—Georgians—were the best horsemen.

According to the noted western historian Dee Brown:

> Trick riding came to rodeo by way of a troupe of Cossack daredevils imported by the 101 Ranch. Intrigued by the Cossacks' stunts on their galloping horses, western cowboys soon introduced variations to American rodeo.

11. All Born Princes

Brown traced a link to the Georgian trick riders that is still found in the present day.

> Colorful costumes seem to be a necessary part of trick riding, and it is quite possible that the outlandish western garb which has invaded rodeo area can be blamed directly on Cossacks and trick riders.[44]

Unknown trick rider.

Another author, Bob Wade, confirms: "Evolving from early Russian circus trick riders, rodeo performers thrilled crowds with 'stands,' 'vaults,' and 'drags.'"[45]

"The Cossack riding was an innovation for the local organization and is in fact practiced by but very few National Guard companies. It was introduced into Syracuse, New York, by John Slack, a former member of the 101 Ranch Wild West show."[46]

Here are some tricks that even nowadays are used in rodeo by cowboy performers: "Lazyback Roll Back," "Cossack, Russian, Suicide, or Death Drag," "Russian Drag Back of the Saddle," "Hippodrome Liberty or Cossack Stand," "Cossack Saddle split," etc.

In the end of the 19th century, "the cowboy [had] already experimented enough to be making flying and running mounts" wrote author Frank E. Dean.

> Most of them knew how to stand in the saddle, some knew how to vault… When the Cossacks came to the United States for the World's Fair in Chicago

Joseph Tsetskhladze (courtesy Buffalo Bill Museum and Grave, Golden, Colorado).

in 1893, the Americans picked up some hints and bright ideas. From that date on, trick riding had a boom from coast to coast. The Russians knew how to tuck to a vault which gave them tremendous spring. They used saddles and straps to help them which the bareback riders had not used. Their horses were saddle horses and they were trained to run straight without swerving, regardless of what gymnastics the rider might be doing. Cowboys went home and gave their ponies a going over. They worked alone and did some inventing and some improving, took some spills, and came up with modern trick riding—which has been unequaled anywhere on earth.[47]

Richard C. Rattenbury stated that rodeo programmers borrowed trick riding from the extravagant equestrian feats of Cossack performers in the Wild West shows.[48]

I have looked through the numerous materials about Georgian trick riders. I knew they were expert horsemen, maybe the best, but I was very surprised when I happened to read rider Nikoloz Chkonia's letter from America, where he states: "You know what a lousy rider I am ... I am perfecting my riding, now I may vault onto or off of a horse while it is in motion, thanks to God in future everything will be all better.... To this moment I can't explain how such amateur rider was employed by the Wild West show managers...."

12. Who's Guilty?

In 1908, when Vasil Amashukeli, a Georgian filmmaker, made his first experimental films, the Georgian cinema was born. Tbilisi, Georgia's capital, celebrated the opening of its first movie theatre in 1896. Started from the early 20th century, Tbilisi boasted as many cinema houses as St. Petersburg and other major cities of the Russian empire.

The number of movie theaters in Georgia was increasing when the Bolsheviks came to power in 1921, for they saw the film industry as a powerful means of propaganda due to its popularity. Communistic restrictions were not as harsh and widespread in the early 1920s, especially after the implementation of the New Economic Policy (NEP). NEP was proposed to prevent the Russian economy from collapsing. That is why the Soviet movie theaters were taken over by the American movies. They were outnumbering the Soviet productions four to one.

In the beginning of the 20th century, the Georgians' adventures in the United States made it to the silver screen. In 1925, one of the pillars of Georgian filmmaking, Alexander Tsutsunava (1881–1955), influenced by American Western movies, made a film, *Who's Guilty?* (another title is *Wild West Rider*), which was based on Nino Nakashidze's play. *Who's Guilty?* was inspired by one trick rider's ill-fated story. It deals with a young farmer Siko (Kote Mikaberidze) who wants to start a new life by working for an American circus. His wife, Pati (Nato Vachnadze), baby, and mother remain in Georgia. After Siko leaves, his child dies. Pati is in despair. The neighbor Isidore seduces Pati; she became pregnant. Meanwhile, Siko's American lover gives birth to their child. After one year of absence, Siko returns home; unable to bear the shame, Pati commits suicide. Siko burns his house and dies.

According to the film historian Giorgi Dolidze,

> After much consideration, Alexander Tsutsunava decided to show an American circus in his film. Unfortunately he was unable to travel to America and with much research still needed, Tsutsunava, accompanied by the actor Kote Mikaberidze, went to his native village Likhauri to visit the Kvitaishvilis'

12. Who's Guilty?

Still from the film *Who's Guilty?* Kote Mikaberidze as Siko.

family. The Kvitaishvilis were the Wild West shows' original participants, performing before the Bolshevik revolution [they would participate in the film along with other trick riders]. As soon as they approached the Kvitaishvilis' house they heard a song coming from a field. Coming closer they realized that the Kvitaishvilis' daughter, who had been born and brought up in America, was singing the song in English. Her parents were accompanying her in English as well. Tsutsunava's visit proved to be a success, and the Kvitaishvilis had much to tell him about the years spent with the Wild West shows.[1]

The film depicts the Georgian riders' virtuosic plasticity and fiery temper in the circus arena. Cheerful and eccentric horsemen from a Georgian village managed to adapt easily to modern rhythms of New York—in "Music Hall," they rhythmically adjust the national dance skills to the foxtrot. They have fun, joke, and surprise people with quick and unexpected movements or fast tricks fitting to jazz-band rhythms.[2] In the first three weeks, 60 thousand spectators attended *Who's Guilty?* According to the magazine *Sovetsky Ekran*, "the best scene of the film

Georgian Trick Riders in American Wild West Shows

is the Wild West show arena. It was unbelievable that the entire set was built by the Georgians.... The cast of the circus was internationally diverse; consequently, all participants tackled the riding technique differently. For instance, the Georgians' riding skills conspicuously differed from that of the cowboys and so on."[3] It should be noted that a huge construction of a circus was built in the pavilion of the Tbilisi studio, and the whole scene in the Wild West Show was filmed in one day. The extras were the citizens of Tbilisi, dressed in European garb, and also some Americans, who worked in those days in Georgia.

Tsutsunava also managed to meet other riders who were living then in Georgia. In a letter dated August 23, 1925, to Ivane Urushadze, the rider Luka Chkhartishvili grumbles about the photos lost by Tsutsunava's assistants.

> I asked them why did they need the photos, and they told me that they were going to show these photos on a screen first in Georgia and then in Russia. I told them that I'd give them the photos only if they put me and my friends' names who had performed in various exhibitions on them, and they agreed

Still from the film *Who's Guilty?*

12. Who's Guilty?

and told me that they needed the photos of 15 men and 4 women, and I was really delighted, but it turned out that they were lying to me. Later I sent Panteleimon Tsintsadze, a friend of mine, to collect the photos and money, but in vain. They promised to send me the photos and money, but I'm still waiting for them. There are two photos there that I wouldn't have agreed to sell even for 200 rubles, and I intended to exhibit them myself, but lack of time was my enemy.

Later, in 1929, the Georgian riders who had performed in various circuses in both sides of the Atlantic also acted in another film by Tsutsunava, called *Mutiny in Guria,* which deals with the famous rebellion in 1841.

Interestingly, tens of thousands of feet of film depict Buffalo Bill's and other shows, among which Cossacks are shown only for few minutes. I have not been able to give a justifiable explanation to this. However, despite this, the riders were incredibly popular, and various articles and magazines suffice to prove it. Perhaps the main reason was the influence of the Russian empire and the negative image that it gave to them. It is possible that due to this very reason, they were not paid enough attention, and had people known who the Cossacks really were, they would have had a different fate and thus we would have had more information and film footage about them. I've heard stories from riders' descendants that the Georgian horsemen worked in Hollywood, appearing in dozens of motion pictures that needed trick riders, often dressed as a cowboy, Indian, cavalry trooper, or whatever the film required. But, still, it is not documented.

13. Gurian Republic and the Outlaw-Pirals

The Russo-Japanese War (1904–1905) became a popular feature in American Wild West shows and helped further taint the image of Russia. The shows pitted Japanese warriors (the underdog) against Cossacks (the Russian giant), and the struggle found an eager audience that generally supported the Japanese.[1] Not only had the audience supported the Japanese, but the American government, too. When in 1904 the Japanese attacked the Russians at Port Arthur, President Roosevelt was delighted—"Japan is playing our game," he wrote to his son.[2]

Pawnee Bill mounted a Russo-Japanese War act in 1904, but was reluctant to take sides between "the mighty Slav race and the Yankees of the East." The *Washington Post* claimed that the crowd failed to applaud the Cossacks and that popular sentiment was on the side of the Japanese, despite the fact that "the plainsmen from Siberia demonstrated their equestrian superiority."[3] "When the Japanese cavalry made their appearance they were loudly cheered, but there was not one to cheer the Czar's Cossacks when they dashed into the arena."[4] This was very unusual for them, because as a rule, the Georgians' every appearance aroused generous and appreciative applause from the public. But now, "Cossacks" were very bad guys. As the announcer set the stage, Luka Chkhartishvili and his men marched across the arena singing. The Japanese fired a volley at close range from an ambush and then opened up with a Maxim gun. The fierce warriors from Russia fled in disorder.

In interview with *The Daily Times*, Alexis Georgian commented on the Russian-Japanese war:

> Captain Alexis Georgian, who has charge of the detachment of Cossacks with the Buckskin Bill Wild West, is an entertaining conversationalist, speaking English and a number of other languages with but a slight accent. Asked this morning if he was going back to fight for Russia he said: "No, we will make the United States our home in the future because we would be con-

13. Gurian Republic and the Outlaw-Pirals

scripted if we went back and we don't want to war against Japan. I feel sorry for the Japanese as there are too many Russian soldiers for them to beat. Russia has all of Europe afraid of her and there will be no intervention by the other powers. If England should interfere she would find France and Germany opposed to her and it would be so if any other country should take up the battle for the Japanese. Russia has a great many more foes within her borders than she has outside of them and the government fully realized this fact but all they can do is to fight internally and externally to the end. We have millions and millions of acres of land in Russia that are unoccupied and should be cultivated, but the condition of the common people is such that they are not able to obtain title to lands or implements to work the lands with and this condition is one that will eventually cause the end of the present form of government in Russia. I feel more sorrow when I think of my own people in Russia."

"Captain Georgian has been in this country several years with different tent exhibitions and he and his compatriots give the lie to the current idea that Cossacks are savages. His men are strong, intelligent and liberty loving and will all make themselves citizens of this country as soon as possible. The Buckskin Bill show has a number of characters on its rolls and a lot of fine men are connected with it.[5]

Georgian horsemen, New York, 1907.

Georgian Trick Riders in American Wild West Shows

In view of the war between Russia and Japan, considerable interest centered in the meeting between the Japanese and the Cossacks who are to appear in the Wild West Show this season. It was feared that racial animosity might be manifested, but happily nothing of the kind was observed, and Major Burke made a point of personally introducing each Japanese to every Cossack inside the waiting-room on the stage. They all shook hands in the most friendly manner, and there is no reason to anticipate any quarrel between these representatives of opposing countries.[6] The Wild West show's one Japanese performer, George Mizuno, talked about Russian-Japanese war: "The Japs will win, sure thing. If they can't win with the soldiers they now have over there, they can send over to this country for us fellows, and we will go over and help give the czar a black eye." Alexis Georgian came up to the group and heard the statement of Japanese. Georgian is a finely built, handsome fellow. A belt full of cartridges added a little to the ferociousness of his appearance. Did the Russian take exception in the remarks of the little Jap? Not a bit of it. He put his right arm around the little Jap's neck and said: "We're good friends, George and I. And the Japs aren't any more anxious to see the Russians get the worst of it than we are. Happy Day for Small Boy."[7]

In the Russo-Japanese War, Russia suffered many great defeats and losses. This humiliated the people of Russia and caused them to lose confidence in Czar Nicholas II, as well as causing great military, economic, and political problems for Russia. This therefore caused the Russo-Japanese War to be partly responsible for the outbreak of the 1905 Revolution.

In 1905, American journalist and author Ernest Poole and his Russian guide Tarasov traveled around Russian Empire to write a series of articles about the Russia for *Outlook* magazine. They visited Tbilisi, Batumi, Kutaisi, and Guria. Ernest Poole recorded his Georgian travels in his book *The Bridge, My Own Story* (1940).

> First we saw only poverty. The children all were weak and thin; no jolly shouts, only dreary silence. The bare cabins looked bleak in fast-thickening rain.
> "Well," I said to Tarasov, "I hope the governor learns of this and has us fired out of here. For all of the cold wet holes on earth."
> "Right, stranger," said a sad-eyed peasant on crutches, who stood close by. "It's a damned dead place for sure."
> "Where in hell did you learn English?"
> "Four years with Buffalo Bill," he replied. "He make me a Cossack in Rough Rider troop and we have one hell of a good time. But I broke my leg bad. So here I am home." He spat sadly into the mud. [This rider possibly was Bartlome Baramidze, who had broken his leg in 1902.] But when I told him why

13. Gurian Republic and the Outlaw-Pirals

I had come, he brightened up. "Good. Write it all your most big papers. How we are poor and why we strike! I will show!" And he took us to peasant huts where all morning we heard their stories of woes.

"Poorer and poorer every year!" one stooping white-headed old peasant declared. "Ever since I was a boy we have been slaves to the landowners here! Always they kept raising the rents, and besides, the judges and priests and police made us pay and pay in bribes, or they would beat us or curse our souls! And as we could do nothing, for we were unarmed! But so at last we decided to strike. We stopped work in their fields and the owners grew angry. They took our cattle! We took them back! And the police and judges shouted: 'This is revolution!'"

"We cannot revolt without any guns," the little village doctor said. "So we outlaw our oppressors instead. We say to the landowners: 'Keep your fields.' And to the governor: 'Stay in your town. We will pay you all your taxes; we will pay for your judges, priests and police. But let the judge sit alone in his court, the priest in his church and the policeman in his jail. We ourselves will settle our disputes, punish our criminals, marry our lovers and bury our dead.' And so we have done. But now this outlawed government in fury has brought the Cossacks here to drive us on to violence, and God only knows how soon it will be till our young hotheads rise with only knives and clubs! For as a doctor night after night I am called to young girls bleeding from rape. Twenty Cossacks had a girl one afternoon a week ago! I could do little! She died last night! They are not men but devils."[8]

After the beginning of the 1905 Revolution, the revolt began spreading throughout Georgia, and the Gurian revolution proceeded even in a more radical way. Guria was known for its oppositionist stance towards the Russian rule; many such rebellions broke out in Guria, in 1841, 1862, and 1886, but Russia always managed to bloodily end them. The Gurians still continued to fight against the restraint of their freedom. In the end of the 19th century, the number of people opposing the Czar's regime was growing rapidly. They always rebelled against injustice and abuse. Together with the restraint of their freedom, the hot-tempered and unyielding Gurian character could not bear witnessing the obnoxious behavior of the Russian governors, perpetual unjust trials, high taxes, poverty, and inability to own land. Some Gurians would take a gun and run into the woods, in order to prove their own truth. Such people were called the pirals. The word pirali is derived from an Arabic word pirar, which means the escaped one. The newspaper *Iveria* (in the second half of the 19th century) wrote: "They [authorities] never asked for reasons why people run to woods. The hunger and poverty are the answers." Not

Georgian Trick Riders in American Wild West Shows

Bartlome Mshvidobadze.

13. Gurian Republic and the Outlaw-Pirals

every Gurian peasant who encountered injustice would escape into the woods, however. Such an action required great physical strength and endurance. That is why a true pirali was the one who was strong, agile, and a courageous and skilled marksman. Often when the disputes

Kirile Pirtskhalaishvili.

between the local government and the peasants would settle down, a peasant would return home and continue a peaceful living with his family. A toast to peace and a corresponding song have always been first at Gurian feasts and carousals.

The Gurian pirals were quite different from ordinary outlaws. They were a kind of Robin Hood. No other outlaw (often even authorities) would ever approach a village from where an outlaw-pirali had escaped. For this reason, pirals were always loved and supported by the people. Even today Guria remembers those legendary pirals for both good and evil deeds. The folk songs about the pirals tell the process by which those in power oppress the common man by making him into an outlaw, tell us about their courage, fearlessness, uprightness. Pirals were memorialized by people with their heroic acts and their sometimes supernatural abilities. For example, pirali and terrorist Datiko Shevardnadze, a granduncle of former president Eduard Shevardnadze, is well known to have had an enchanted body, so that he could not be killed by bullets.

I have heard the stories firsthand from a number of old-time Gurians about the trick riders who, after homecoming, supposedly became involved in Revolutionary movement and became pirali-outlaws. One of these stories is connected with Silibistro Makharadze, Ivane's brother, who in 1907 helped a well-known pirali and terrorist, wanted by the police, to escape—Melqisedek Guntaishvili. Before Guntaishvili and his comrades escaped, a fight occurred, and one policeman was killed. The policeman's brother-in-law blamed Silibistro for everything that happened. Police began to hunt for him. Silibistro had no other chance but to hide out in the forest.

One year later, Silibistro's eldest daughter planned to get married. The escapee decided to come home for the wedding. The mamasakhlisi (village head) informed the police about Silibistro's presence. During the feast, armed men came for Silibistro. He tried to escape, but was killed.

In the beginning of the 1900s, Marxist ideas spread throughout Georgia. The Russian Social Democratic Labour Party (RSDLP) took control of the Georgian nationalist movement. The popularity and spread of Social Democratic activity in Georgia became apparent after the peasant movement in Guria started in the spring of 1902. Gurian peasants initiated sowing strikes; several Georgian Social Democrats

13. Gurian Republic and the Outlaw-Pirals

Nikoloz Surguladze and his family (photomontage made by Surguladze).

supported the peasants; several committees were established under the Caucasus League of the RSDLP; and the peasant movement prevailed outside Guria and joined the labor movements in cities. The population of Western Georgia and Guria in particular was politically more active than that of the eastern part of the country. It must be mentioned that almost all the leaders of the short-lived Georgian Democratic Republic (1918–1921), which was established after the October Revolution of 1917, were from Guria: Noe Jordania, Noe Ramishvili, Benia Chkhikvishvili (the latter was the "President" of "Gurian Republic"), Grigol Uratadze. Gurians has been putting the theories of into practice, defying the Russian Government, and refusing to recognize any authority but their own.

Gurians would never collaborate with the Russian execution teams in the villages. If someone did, the revenge would be terrible; this person or persons would be boycotted. This form of protest was first used in England in the opposition between the peasants and the landlords. Boycott was wide spread in revolutionary Guria. Everyone feared the boycott, because in this case the person would be isolated from society, from neighbors. "The supreme punishment by boycott was such: a guilty person was not allowed to leave the yard and no one was permitted to come to him, even in case his house appeared to be on fire; there were cases when the family members were not given the right to talk to the punished. I remember cases when the guilty was punished with a bullet. All these punishments were passed by people at mass meetings," wrote an anonym author. Often pallbearers refused to carry coffins of the boycotted; gravediggers refused to bury them.

As a result of their boycott by the Georgian peasantry, all local bureaucratic institutions had ground to a halt, and in their stead under the aegis of the Social Democrats, there had emerged a whole new infrastructure of self-administration to which the whole population deferred: elected land committees set the appropriate rates for rent paid by the peasants for land they leased from local landowners; elected committees had taken complete charge of local school matters, including the hiring of the teachers and the setting of curricula; elected judges and popular assemblies acting as ultimate courts of appeal settled the most varied types of disputes, from land claims to marital conflicts. Guria became a separate region where police power could not enter. "Once we had left the railway," wrote Luigi Villari, "behind us all anxiety as to the danger

13. Gurian Republic and the Outlaw-Pirals

of arrest was at an end, for we were now in free Guria, where the Russian writ no longer runs, and gendarmes, politzmeisters, pristavs, and such-like gentry are but vain things."[9] The emergence of this new structure of effective authority, even before the overthrow of autocracy, reflected a mobilization of popular support by social democracy unparalleled anywhere else in Russian Empire. It was known as "Gurian Republic," which went under the flag of the Social Democrats, later Mensheviks. This term used to indicate the revolutionary events that took place in Guria prior to and during 1905 Russian Revolution. The success of the Gurian Republic was not due to the strength of Marx's ideas. The Gurian peasants were religious believers who swore oaths on icons.[10] From Guria, the revolutionary fever spread with lightning rapidity into neighboring Imereti and Mingrelia and the whole of Georgia.

It is interesting to note that that one of the great advances of Gurian Republic was the disappearance of robbers. Georgian newspaper *Mogzauri* (1905, #1) quoted: "Thieving and other crimes have not been totally extinguished, but have almost completely disappeared. Punishments are, in most cases, rather psychological ones. The Kutaisi province, having been infamous for thieving and robbery, has been completely transformed now, after people ceased to rely on government organizations, and dealt with their own problems by themselves."

On October 20, 1905, a clash between a 120-Cossack detachment under the head of

Sergi Gvarjaladze.

district Lazarenko and armed peasants in Nasakirali, Guria, resulted in fourteen Cossacks being killed. Authorities ordered Major General Alikhanov-Avarsky to restore order; Western Georgia, particularly Guria, was devastated by Russian Cossacks. Here is a quote of one Russian officer who was sent in to Georgia on a punitive expedition, when the Caucasian administration declared martial law: "They sent us to the sword and fire to win the Caucasus.... We will drink, like this cup of wine, Georgians' blood." They burned numerous towns and villages, killed hundreds of innocent women, children and men; 13,000 people were arrested, and many of them were sentenced to death, to hard labor, and to exile in Siberia. The "Gurian Republic," which lasted six months, was drowned in blood. This was the end.

14. Life and Times of the Wild West

For the most part, the Georgians interacted well with the representatives of other nations whom they encountered during show business. But not always.

> It happened in May. We began our daily exercises when Mexicans and cowboys approached us and offered to compete against us. We agreed... After a signal we started the competition, but in the second racecourse they fell far behind... They became infuriated and started shouting and scolding us, but how could that help them? A cowboy named Lyle who was not participating in the show followed Aristo and struck him with his whip. Poor Aristo somehow managed to stay in the saddle. "What are you doing?" he shouted, but the cowboy struck him again with his whip. Aristo flew off his handle and hit Lyle's head with the handle of his whip. Lyle fell down from his horse... His friends ran up and encircled us. All of them had guns, while we had only whips. We thought the end was near, but suddenly the manager of the show appeared and separated us. Later on they realized their mistake and we made up with them.

Competition sometimes got the best of show folk, but the Georgians were levelheaded and mainly kept to themselves. Frida Mgaloblishvili stated, "We don't socialize a lot with others and it has nothing to do with our arrogance. It's a sort of a custom to cling to each other." (Quote from the unidentified English-language newspaper.)

The language barrier was an issue, as well, but even that didn't prevent the Georgians from forming friendships.

> During the Boer War, a number of wounded Boers were invited to join the circuses. Boers were the Americans' favorites and they used to attract huge audiences. While they performed for Buffalo Bill's Wild West show they stayed away from cowboys and Mexicans and kept company only with the Gurians. They even used to eat dinner together though they couldn't even talk because of the language barrier.[1]

One newspaper describes the day in the rough riders' camp: "It was very amusing to see Arabs chumming with Mexicans and taking lessons

Gurians with Native American.

in lasso throwing. Indians promenading solemnly about with Cossacks, neither able to talk to each other except in the sign language...."[2]

One American newspaper reports on this. "Everyone in the show got along like one big family. The main exception was the objection of the cowboys to the Russian Cossacks, who mistreated their horses and really caused an ill feeling with many who dearly loved their horses." Charles Campbell of Campbell Bros. commented,

> Cossacks are cruel, they maltreated their horses and are held in contempt... They incite the contempt of every performer in the circus. They have absolutely no feeling for their horses, using fine wisps of wire for whips which cut the hides and will drive a pointed spur into a horse's side until the blood spurts out. They kill more horses than any troupe of performers on the road, and there is no such a thing as stopping their cruelties, if you desire to keep them with the circus.[3]

In spite of this the Campbell Bros. kept "Cossacks" in their show until it went bankrupt in 1912. It must be noted here that the Georgians didn't use spurs, which indeed are very painful to horses; they wore soft leather riding boots and used whips. Author Richard J. Walsh, when he described[4] the Georgians' dress, had mentioned "top boots with silver

14. Life and Times of the Wild West

spurs"; this was confirmed by Jill Jonnes, the author of the book *The Eiffel's Tower and the World's Fair Where Buffalo Bill Beguiled*.[5] As I understand, it was "parade" attire, and it's visibly shown in the photos.

On the whole, the Georgians were treated with friendliness.

> Some of the Cossacks who are with the Campbell show have familiar faces. They were residents of the city for several months two years ago. It was interesting to watch one of them as he came up the street. The first familiar face he met was Ed Sutherland and the meeting was almost as pathetic as that of a Prodigal son and his father. The Cossack hung upon "Pipe's" neck in a most affectionate manner.[6]

The riders of various ethnic origins usually were companionable when their paths crossed. An unknown Gurian rider commented on a fistfight that took place between him and one guy.

> I met a charming girl, whose name was Mary Lou ... I used to call her Maniko. An Italian guy claimed that she was his girlfriend, but she told him that everything was over between them. The guy became furious and would not leave her alone, so I asked him if he had heard what Maniko had said.

Gurians and Native Americans.

He shouted something at me in Italian and then punched me in the eye. He thought I would fall down, but I punched him back and knocked out some of his teeth. It was real fighting. Finally, they managed to separate us.

Another fight with an Italian was described by the *Brooklyn Daily Eagle* (May 6, 1902). Near the entrance to the Wild West show, in Brooklyn, New York, a cowboy named "Wild Bill" endeavored to help himself to some peanuts from an Italian vendor, but refused to pay. The enraged vendor stabbed the cowboy with a stiletto knife. The newspaper reported:

> The other cowboys, the two Indians who were in their war paint ready for the afternoon performance, the two Cossacks, and the Mexican vaqueros forgot their race difference for the moment and rushed to Wild Bill's assistance. One of the Mexicans let go a lasso he carried. He missed the Italian, but he caught the peanut stand, which, with a crash, was overturned and deposited its contents on the Halsey street car tracks.

The row ended when the injured cowboy was taken into the doctor's tent. No arrests were made.

Left to right: **Silovan Kartvelishvili, Simon Oragvelidze, Pavle Makharadze, Edinburgh, 1904.**

14. Life and Times of the Wild West

I have Buffalo Bill's cabinet photo, and on the back, one rider, to whom it belonged, made an inscription: "Cody—he's our master." "Yes, said the Prince, the Colonel is very popular with our party. He has the respect of the Cossacks as well as of all the rest of the performers."[7] Famous Annie Oakley, who worked on Buffalo Bill's Wild West for seventeen years, said of Cody: "There were thousands of men in the outfit during that time. Comanches, cowboys, Cossacks, Arabs, and every kind of person. And the whole time we were one great family loyal to a man."[8]

The *Newcastle Guardian* (April 23, 1904) describes the arrival of Cody and his troupe in England:

> Colonel Cody and the greater part of his staff reached Liverpool on Saturday night late in the *Lucania*. They were a day late, owing to the circumstances of the vessel being delayed at New York some 16 hours longer than she should have been owing to fog. A large crowd had gathered to witness the debarkation of Colonel W. F. Cody and his plainsmen, a centre of attraction being a group of Cossacks, who reached England a couple of days ago from the Caucasus and came to Liverpool to welcome their "father" (as they call Buffalo Bill) and their international comrades from the West. The Cossacks displayed the Union Jack and the Stars and Stripes with a banner of "Welcome," and broke into hearty cheers as the *Lucania* came alongside with the Wild West members grouped on deck. The Indians burst into one of their weird chants, the Cowboy Band under Professor William Sweeney played "Hiawatha," and as the ship was made fast, pealed out the "Star-Spangled Banner," followed by the British National Anthem. General cheering greeted Colonel Cody as the fine upright figure of the famous scout became visible near the gangway. Following Colonel Cody off the ship came the cowboys, 50 Red Indians in beaded blankets and eagle feather war bonnets, Mexican vaqueros, in their picturesque national costume, and, equally interesting, a dozen Japanese, who came from the Mikado's country via San Francisco.

This event was drawn by well-known magazine illustrator Ernest Prater, who was commissioned by Major Burke to make sketches of the "boss" and the performers. The sketches were then copied by newspapers and magazines.

Author Alan Gallop, in his book *Buffalo Bill's British Wild West*, made a quotation of Buffalo Bill Cody's sincere farewell speech to his troupe after the final performance in 1903.

> Once more we are closing one of our many seasons and I want to compliment members of the company for their loyalty to their duty and uncomplaining work throughout these months of rain and mud. I want to say that I hope in the spring to meet many familiar faces back in the arena.

Georgian Trick Riders in American Wild West Shows

You are now about to depart to your various homes, a journey which takes you many thousands of miles apart. I am in hope that you will occasionally remember the season of 1903 in good old loyal England (cheers from the company) where we have been treated so kindly by everyone we have come

Ilarion Ebralidze.

14. Life and Times of the Wild West

into contact with. I have no hesitations in saying that there are no more loyal people under the sun than the English people. I know that you join me in heartfelt thanks to His Majesty the King and Her Majesty the Queen of England, both of whom came to see the performance while we were in London (more cheers from the company).

Although it has been a very rainy season, we have had less sickness in our company than we have had for many years, even in America. It has been very disagreeable at times—very disagreeable—and we have all longed for the sunshine that did not come very often (laughter from the company). I do not think that will prevent us from coming back to try again another year (cries of "hurrah" from the company).

I hope you all reach your homes in health, that you will get a good rest and you will enjoy yourselves in whatever occupation you take up. You will have my kindest regards and sympathy for your welfare and your health. (Lusty cheers, cowboy calls, war whoops and yells of appreciation in many different tongues and keys.)[9]

Although very popular, Buffalo Bill ruled his troupe with an iron fist, something necessary because of the ill will among the nations represented in the show.[10] According to *The New York Times,* April 7, 1901, Wild West general manager and chief press agent Major Burke's duty was to make friends for the show. "He tries to keep everybody in a good humor, from the broken-down characters who seek tickets to the Indians who are disaffected toward Russian Cossacks." It is proven by one incident that took place in Port Jervis (Orange County, New York).

After the performance of Buffalo Bill's Wild West, many of the Indi-

Theodore Roosevelt's tray, which was given to Giorgi Chkhaidze.

ans and others connected with the show wandered about town, seeing the sights and making purchases. While the horses and paraphernalia of the exhibition were being placed on the Erie Railroad cars, six Indians and three Cossacks entered a saloon and drank freely. The convivial party was executing a war dance when in walked Mr. Cody. There is little ceremony about the measures taken by the leading spirit of the Wild West. He kicked the Cossacks out of the place, it is said, and drawing a revolver ordered the Indians to leave; they left. Mr. Cody then reprimanded the barkeeper for selling liquor to the red men, calling his attention to its prohibition by the government.[11]

When Salsbury asked about liquor, he replied: "No drink is allowed to be sold in the camp to any of our men, and we have Indians here whom you could not force to take liquor. But all know it is the rule of the camp, and knowing that they submit without a murmur."[12] However, several Native American performers ultimately had to be dismissed from the show because of their alcoholic tendencies. An unknown Gurian rider talks about Indians and their predisposition to drinking: "Indians love to drink too much and some of them can drink their whiskey as Russians and lose their mind. Their drunkenness is excessive."

Giorgi Chkhaidze.

It was not uncommon for princes, kings, and other royals to attend the Wild West shows, including Presidents Woodrow Wilson and Theodore Roosevelt. The latter, a Spanish-American war hero, outdoorsman, and rough rider, attended a show in Chicago and was so fascinated by Giorgi Chkaidze's performance that he presented him with a golden ring and a tray as a token of his esteem. "It was so big that it nearly covered my finger," recalled Chkaidze. According to Chkaidze's daughter Ekaterine, her father had to sell the ring to escape prison after coming back to Georgia. The reason for that was the fact that Chkhaidze talked much about the lifestyle and brilliance of foreign countries, especially America, and that was prohibited in those Soviet times. Thus the information reached the Bolsheviks, who ordered him to be imprisoned. The family was forced to sell the ring to pay for his freedom.

The riders, in turn, had a chance to visit the White House: Alexis Georgian attended President McKinley's reception in honor of Pawnee Bill; Dimitri and Frida Mgaloblishvilis were received by President Cleveland; Pawnee Bill, Alexis Georgian, and other chiefs called on President McKinley and were warmly received with handshakes; Ivane Makharadze Major Burke, two Sioux Indian Chiefs, and Tom Oliver were invited by the Duke of Orleans to the Savage Club.

In May, 1914, Prince Luka and his "Cossacks," members of the 101 Ranch Real Wild West, performed in England.

> Queen Alexandra of England, accompanied by the Empress Marie of Russia, the Princess Royal, and her daughter, Princess Maud, sat in the royal boxes when the Millers took a bow and then proceeded to stage the most stupendous wild west performance the old world had ever seen. Soon after the royal party arrived, dozens of cowboys, cowgirls, and Indians appeared in the arena uttering their wild cries as they cantered round at breakneck pace. Then came pioneer scouts and an emigrant train. Claims were "staked out," and Wild West sports took place. A display of riding by the Russian Cossacks particularly pleased the Empress Marie, who pointed out all the details of their costume to her sister. Some remarkable rifle shooting on horseback also excited the admiration of the royal party. Queen Alexandra, who was dressed in black with a small black net hat and a red rose in her blouse, remained for an hour and a half and evidenced much interest in the performances, as the following lines reveal:
>
> Queen Alexandra yesterday afternoon paid a visit to the Anglo-American Exhibition at Shepherd's-bush for the primary purpose of witnessing the "Wild West" performance given within the Stadium. In four motor-cars her Majesty and the party by whom she was accompanied set out from Marlborough House shortly after three o'clock. In the first car were Queen Alexandra herself and the Empress Marie of Russia, attended by Sir Colin Keppel; in the second were the Princess Royal and her daughter, Princess Maud, together with the Hon. Violet Vivian; the third car accommodated the

Georgian Trick Riders in American Wild West Shows

Countess of Antrim, Colonel Streatfield, Prince Chervachidze, and Countess Mengden; and seated in the fourth were General Sir Dighton Probyn and the Hon. Charlotte Knollys.[13]

Chervachidze (must be Shervashidze) was of a Georgian ruling family of the Principality of Apkhazeti (Abkhazia). The Prince might be Giorgi. There is no information whether compatriots Shervashidze and the Georgians had a meeting after the performance.

When free of touring, the Gurian riders did their best to have the time of their lives in the United States. The press never missed a chance to track them down, while they were riding, playing poker, or flirting.

Georgian horsemen, United States, circa 1903.

14. Life and Times of the Wild West

"The Cossacks still remain with us but they have 'dough.' A poker party took place recently in which the Slavs took part. They had $300 in gold on the table." On May 5, 1907, *The Saint Louis Daily Globe Democrat* wrote that Prince Luka Chkhartishvili had been elected the president of a golf club, "The Lillie Paws," that included eight members of Pawnee Bill's Far East show: A Senegalese musician, a Dahomeyan chieftain, a Hindu magician, Luka, a captain of Moorish infantry, a warrior from the South Sea Islands, an Arab acrobat, and an Australian bushman. "The club took its name from a combination of Pawnee Bill's professional title and his name in private life, where he is known as Major Gordon W. Lillie. The president of the club is Prince Luka, the colonel of the Cossacks. He is a veteran of the late Japanese-Russian war, and as such is honored by his associates."

These exotic Georgian riders also made an impression on the fairer sex in America and Europe. "We are much respected here, especially by ladies," said one Gurian rider. "One wealthy American woman even offered a friend of ours to marry her, but the poor bastard chose to tie the knot with a Georgian lady, and now he relishes all the inconveniences of life in Guria." *The Evening News Michigan* (August 12, 1899) reported: "A handsome Cossack stopped as he wrung the

Iason Imnadze.

water from his close cropped pointed beard and waved a graceful salute, his gleaming teeth showing through his fascinating smile. The girls giggled, turned their heads, then looked back again, and hesitating a second, wiggled their flirtatious fingers. The gallant Cossack bowed low."

Some Georgians wed the Americans ladies and settled down in the United States. "One local lady woman clung to Alexander, she insisted that he marry her … at first he was against the idea, but later he agreed and married her. He left the show and now he lives in California with his wife." As *The Elgin Courant & Courier* (September 2, 1904) stated, "The Cossacks have a high opinion of Elgin[14] and its people. One young Russian gentleman was quite enthusiastic about it, and said Elgin was very beautiful, there were good men and women and nice girls, the latter remark being accompanied with broad grin." Still, there were some riders who entered into marriage bonds with the American ladies and settled down there. In one case, a married rider wedded an American woman and returned to Georgia after a while. But when he was about to go back to the States, the Bolsheviks wouldn't let him out of the country and he committed suicide. In another case, an American lady gave a rider a huge golden ring as a token of her affection to wear on his penis.

15. The Death Race

Tragic cases were commonplace at the Wild West shows. The riders often risked breaking their necks while touring. They were skilled performers, but the dangers of their business were real. *The Washington Post* describes an incident that took place on October 3, 1895.

> It was just as the Cossacks were retiring on a run that one of their horses fell. He and his rider rolled in a cloud of dust under the feet of the others. One Cossack jumped his horse over the two fallen ones, and the dismounted man springing to his feet was almost run down by another rider behind him but apparently the Russians are made of rubber and whale bone, for the dismounted man instead of being carried out to the hospital jumped up and chased his horse out of the arena on foot and nearly caught him.

Who can count how often they used to break their arms and legs after such accidents? Some riders were not lucky or long-lived. It is said that in about 1903, Polta Tsintsadze died in a very ambiguous situation on board a ship entering the port of New York. Some said that he was poisoned by rider Baramidze. Tsintsadze was buried somewhere in New York.

The Buffalo Courier (July 15, 1901) wrote: "The riding of the Cossacks is wonderful, but by reason of the heavy, unwieldy saddle is not as clean cut as the exhibitions of the Americans. Last night a horse ridden by one of the Russians fell while going at full speed and slid for some distance, when it regained its feet and dashed on, the rider in his saddle."

The Indianapolis Star (August 27, 1907) reported: "Hundreds of horses raced round and round the big arena at breakneck speed, with shouting riders in all sorts of positions, yet only one accident occurred to put an extra thrill to the afternoon performance. Nymi Christus [his real name is unknown], Russian Cossack, was thrown to the ground and underneath his horse when the animal, at top speed, stumbled and fell. Christus was carried away to the dressing tent, lifeless, many spectators thought, but he was only stunned." *The Indianapolis News* (August 27, 1907) continued the story: "Everyone for whom the audience had sym-

Nikoloz Antadze on horseback.

pathy was saved except one Cossack, who fell from his horse at the afternoon performance. This Cossack, Nymi Christus by name, was stunned by his fall, and was carried off the field. In the evening another Cossack fell from his horse, but he jumped up and ran off himself."

On October 28, 1907, an unknown Georgian rider died during a performance of Pawnee Bill's Wild West Show in Amarillo, Texas:

15. The Death Race

"Prince Luka's band of Russian Cossacks gave an exhibition of acrobatic and daring horsemanship that was grand and spectacular. Since the little Japs made the fierce Cossacks look so cheap during the late hostilities, the populace don't warm up to them as they once did. One of the most skillful of the Russian riders died yesterday in Amarillo, and this cast a gloom over the entire Russian colony."[1]

The Saint Paul Pioneer Press (June 16, 1908) describes the fall of "Cossack" Sergi Jorbenadze:

> Dashing around the ring at the 101 Wild West show yesterday afternoon, performing his most difficult feat, one which none of the others dare do, Sergi Jorbenadze, the best of the Cossack riders, leaned a little too far out in his stirrups, causing his horse to miss its footing and fall, carrying him underneath. Several men and women in the grandstand fainted. When the rider crawled from beneath his horse, he limped to the animal's side and then collapsed. He was carried out on a stretcher, his leg being broken. The horse, prancing and pawing on three legs, one of its forelegs helplessly dangling, was led from the ground behind the big curtain and shot. Its foreleg was broken.

Ilarion Imnadze, 1912.

On August 29, 1909, Luka Chkhartishvili's brother Michael was badly wounded in Davenport, Iowa.

> One of the Cossacks was nearly dragged to death at Davenport, Iowa, when his horse stumbled. The Cossack was hanging from the saddle by one foot as the horse sped around the arena at full speed. Then the horse fell. The unfortunate man was underneath the animal, and when the equine rose and resumed his mad charge, he was dragged along the ground for many yards before the horse could be pulled down. The rider was unconscious and his leg was twisted, torn, and broken. Prince Lucca, the Cossack Chief, fractured his shoulder in a fall on the slippery, rain-swept ground at Fort Worth later in the season.[2]

In the hospital it was found that he had fractured his leg badly, and he would not be able to continue with the troupe for some time.

Mary Campbell, wife of the Campbell Brothers show owner, recalls a case when a Cossack fell on his own saber and was seriously wounded. Frank Dean mentioned that original Russian Cossacks did their tricks complete with caracul fur hat, long military coat, and ornate dagger swinging from the belt, and some even carried a saber between their teeth. Of the original group who came to the United States, four met a gruesome death because of this billowy uniform. He didn't mention their names, but warned the American trick riders should "benefit by the experience of these Cossacks and wear shirts and saddle pants that allow freedom of action."[3]

In 1912, *The Evening Times* ran a story about Cossack Steve Graceley's death. George Heeney, a friend of Graceley's, was demonstrating a challenging trick. Heeney was riding with one leg thrown over the saddle, the other in the stirrup, and his body straight out from the body of the horse and parallel to the ground. In rounding the turn in the front of the reserved seating stand, the horse slipped and horse and rider went to the ground. Heeney lay still until a cowboy came up and companions threw him across the back of the cowboy's horse, and he was trotted from the arena. So coolly was it done that nearly everyone in the audience thought it was part of the performance. After some time Graceley, who had been in the riding business for 12 years, tried the same trick during a performance and fell from his horse and was admitted to the hospital, where he died on May 26. According to the reporting journalist, he was 38. Graceley was buried at Cumberland Cemetery. Soon after his death, Alexis Georgian informed journalists that Graceley's real name was Irakli

15. The Death Race

Tsintsadze and he was 52. He had no relatives in America and apparently was deep in financial trouble; his friends had to collect the money for his funeral and family. They managed to raise $84; $40 was spent on Tsintsadze's burial, the remainder sent to his widow and six children.

The Georgians took on nicknames because their real names mostly were unpronounceable to the show's organizers and the public. The Georgians appropriated American names, and unfortunately, to this day, many of their names cannot be discovered in the real Georgian. "The Cossacks are not a heterogeneous lot of bewhiskered horsemen gotten together indiscriminately, but learned to ride in their peculiarly daring fashion in the South of Russia, their native land. Their names on the salary roll give unmistakable evidence of their foreign origin. One is Dimitri Mgaloblishvili, another Luka Chkhartishvili. Their chief does not even attempt to pronounce these names. He designates each of his troupe by a number."[4] Alexis Georgian must get his due for identifying Irakli Tsintsadze for us. The same can be said about George Heeney, who was, reportedly, one of the "Cossacks." The list goes on.

At Louisa, Kentucky, on Saturday, October 10, before the beginning of the afternoon performance, Khalampri Pataraia was murdered. From the various newspapers accounts, here is what happened:

> October 10, 1914, the Kit Carson Wild West was in Louisa, Kentucky. It was a Saturday and was raining. A lady (Mrs. Alien Kirk, sister of attorney W.

Khalampri Pataraia.

T. Cain) on one side of the arena wanted to get an umbrella from her brother who was on the other side of the arena. She crossed over and when she got to the other side a Cowboy and Cossack were at the entrance and asked her for her ticket of twenty-five cents… The Cossack could speak no English, except perhaps a few words, "ticket," "quarter," etc. Mr. Cain saw that Mrs. Kirk was trying to get in and went to her, leading her into the seats. A controversy resulted and Cain struck an American showman. The Cossack had followed several steps when Cain turned and struck him with an umbrella … and the Cossack stuck back with his riding whip. The crowd was standing on the seats watching the fight break out. The Cossack left and was bending over to crawl under the canvas flap to get out of the arena when a Mr. Nathan C. Day shot him in the back. The wounded man was hurried to hospital for treatment, the operation requiring much time. The physicians testified that the ball entered an inch and a half on the left of the spine and was removed at a point near the center in front, about the end of the breast bone, and almost on a level with the wound in the back. The patient came out from under the influence of the anesthetic all right and rallied well but he began to sink a few hours later and died about 7:00 o'clock Sunday morning… The Russian consulate was notified by wire of the man's death soon after it occurred…

The strongest witnesses for the defense, Elva Wellman and Al Wellman, swore the Russian drew a long knife just before he was shot. Elva swore he was holding the knife in a threatening manner when shot and that he dropped it as he fell and a stranger ran up and picked up the knife and ran away with it. Al Wellman swore the Cossack was about eight feet from Mr. Day and drew a knife and was "makin at" Day when he shot. He said he saw nothing more of the knife after the man fell … "Jimmie the Cossack," another Russian working in the riding act with the man who was killed, testified as to his dying statement, which was that when the shot struck him he was just in the act of stooping to raise the tent and get out of there. Jimmie swore the man had no knife, but wore only a sword and whip. Nathan C. Day, a hotel proprietor, was convicted January 21, 1915, and given 21 years in prison.[5]

The name of the "Cossack" was Khalampri Pataraia. He was thirty-six years old and had a wife and four children in Guria.

Aggressive masculinity prevailed in the entertainment and in its camp. All the participants of the show, whether cowboys, Indians, Arabs, or Mexicans, used to tell journalists fictitious stories about themselves, which they would fill with blood and gore: an Indian told tales of scalping; an Arab related how he had won his wife by decapitating a rival suitor.[6] The Gurians were no exception. Luka Chkhartishvili told a story to several newspapers of how he killed Don Cossacks:

15. The Death Race

The hottest fight of the Prince's life occurred some six years ago. In it he killed five men and wounded more than a dozen others.

There was a game of ball (a Cossack adaption of America's national game) between a picked team from each of the Prince's principal villages. [It might be Lelo Burti—Field ball—which is a full contact ball game, and very similar to rugby. The two teams, usually consisting of the male population of neighboring villages, would face each other.] Prince Loucas was, of course, umpire. His conduct on that occasion is a shining example to the umpires of the League.

About fifty Don Cossacks, who happened to be in that part of Russia, went to the field to see the game ... the Don Cossacks ... were ugly and disposed to make trouble. They hooted and yelled, and finally ventured so far as to hiss a close decision of the royal umpires.

Prince Luka and his "Cossacks."

Sio Nakaidze, captain of the prince's body-guard, who was twice decorated by Alexander III for conspicuous bravery, became furious and stuck the leader of the Don Cossacks in the face.

A free fight followed.

The Don Cossacks were desperadoes, but the Prince's followers outnumbered them. During the pitched battle several men were killed on both sides, and it was apparent that the fight would be still bloodier.

One of the Don Cossacks waved his white cloak aloft in token of temporary truce. The leader of the strangers proposed that the rest of the battle should be determined by single combat. He and the Prince would fight single-handed, and the first to fall should be succeeded by one of his men, and so on, until one side or the other had been wiped out.

Prince Loucas spurred his horse to the center of the space between the opposing lines, waving his sabre aloft. He soon dispatched the chief of the invading force and killed four more of the Don Cossacks in quick succession, receiving scarcely a scratch.

When the fifth of their number had been killed by the Prince the Don Cossacks lowered their lances in acknowledgment of defeat and rode away toward the setting sun.

Prince Loucas is now called the preserver of his people, and is venerated only less than the Little Father himself.

Luka mentioned a different number of Cossacks in different versions of the story, with the number varying between one and twenty.[7]

Despite these tales of violence, the Georgians usually tried to behave their best in America. But every culture has bad seeds, and so occasionally, reports would crop up, like this from *Arkansas Democrat*, reporting on October 21, 1901:

> One of the "marvelous Imperial Russian Cossacks from the steppes of Russia" of Pawnee Bill's Wild West filled up on red liquor this morning and created consternation in Muller's Saloon at 8:30 o'clock. He resented the efforts of three of his clansmen to remove him to the show grounds, and drawing his murderous double-edged sword, "their principal weapon, which they wield with an expertness that is marvelous," he proceeded to drive them out of the saloon, other patrons scattering by common instinct before his terrific onslaught. The bartender, Carle King, ran to the sidewalk and called an officer. Deputy Constable R.R. King responded and grabbed the malcontent from the steppes, who essayed to draw his sword upon the officer. Then Constable Jones and Detective Spight reinforced him and the three marched to jail the boozy member of "the first genuine contingent of Russia's noted Light Horse Cavalry, in all the regalia of "handsome but somber uniforms." There he will be permitted to sober up sufficiently to answer to the charge of disturbing the peace. His name is another matter. No one could distinguish

15. The Death Race

it from his drunken guttural, and "Theford" was the nearest the linguists of the constabulary could go it.

Presumably this Cossack was Teophane Kavtaradze.

The *Brooklyn Daily Eagle* (August 1, 1902) reported that Buffalo Bill's Wild West show Cossack riders "desperate characters" Frank Schultz and J. Dietreich, "who cleaned out a place at Woodside of $750 worth of jewelry" were captured. Schultz got twenty-two and Dietrich eighteen years. It is still unclear if they were Georgians with Americanized names or not.

Most "incidents" involving Georgians were more like the one rider Giorgi Chkhaidze shared: once the Gurians passed by some wonderful apple orchards. One of them jumped over the fence, picked some apples, and gave them to his friends. The next day an article describing some

Teophane Kavtaradze.

Cossacks who had stolen apples was published in a newspaper. Chkhaidze recalled that they were so ashamed that they would not even go out. In Guria nobody would have said a word about a few apples, but in the United States the media was looking for sensational stories concerning anything related to the Cossacks. Those stories often were untrue. The *New York Clipper* (May 25, 1895) declared that, at Poughkeepsie, a boy was killed in the parade by one of the Cossacks riding over him. In reality, the boy, seven years old, with his mother was watching the parade when one uncontrollable Mexican mustang broke away and plunged into the crowd. The boy was knocked down and cut badly on the head.

16. Prince Luka: Russia's Famous Player

Though the public equally respected all Georgian riders, there also were favorites who were treated as larger-than-life-heroes. Luka Chkhartishvili was definitely one of these. Luka had always been in the media spotlight, but this "fairy tale" article printed in *The Times* (Kansas City, October 19, 1896) surpassed all expectations:

> The Russians are a troupe of Cossacks of the Volga, headed by Prince Luka Chkhartishvili, about whom there is extant probably as pretty a romance as ever was written. The prince, who by the way talks English, French, and German, as well as Russian, is not of the blood royal, although of unquestioned birth and rank. But in his early days he fell in love with Princess Stephanik, the morganatic daughter of the present Czar's father. She returned his love, and in secret they planned to flee to Poland and there live in disguise. Even the night for the elopement was set, and the Prince, who resided in a country palace some miles from St. Petersburg, had started for his bride-to-be, when arrested. The rigid system of passports prevalent in Russia had trapped him. He was banished to Siberia for life and drafted into the military service of the Cossack guards. He had proven himself a brave soldier, and has risen to rank and fame. The Princess died the month after he was banished. With him here are a dozen or more of his fellow soldiers, with curious dress, their long guns, their cartridge belts across their breasts and their queer language.

As the saying is, no comments.

The Morning Journal (May 20, 1894) described Luka: "Prince Loucas is a small man, but much stronger than any of his followers, though some of the latter are six feet six. He is a foot shorter than that height, but he has the shoulders of an ox, and the arms and legs of a Hercules." According to the Georgian newspaper *Kvali* (March 9, 1897), "His exceptional riding skills make him incomparable; all marvel how this man became so consummate in his native village." Prince Luka arrived on the scene in 1892 and performed until the beginning of the First World War. Teophane Kavtaradze was the only rider with greater longevity than Luka. He first emerged at Pawnee Bill's show in 1900 and finished performing in 1925 with the Miller Brothers; his nickname was "Russian Demon." In the show arena, his call was "Hey ho, I am Prince Tepho!"

By origin, Luka was a goldsmith from a relatively well-off family. Despite this, he was illiterate (he couldn't even sign his name in a passport), though later he not only learned how to read and write in Georgian, but mastered English as well. Again, *Tsnobis Purtsely* reported on this, "Sadly, nearly all of them are illiterate except two or three who can manage some Russian. Only one can speak English that he learned while touring in the United States; his name is Luka Chkhartishvili. The riders feel that their illiteracy creates obstacles for them and often grumble about it. One rider, who previously ignored chances to study English abroad, is determined to attend free courses after going back to the States." Many riders were taking English lessons. Classes usually were held in the dressing tent.

The *Brooklyn Citizen* (July, 4, 1894) published a long article about Luka:

> If there are any young women in Brooklyn who are anxious to meet a real live prince there is an opportunity for them almost at their own doors. Frank Small, of the Wild West show, will act as introducer. The prince, who is a very modest man, is married, however, so there is no chance for any weak-minded girl to gather in a title, even if there should be such a young woman in the city. His highness is Prince Loucas Tchkarectrile, of the Province of Launtckouta, Russian Caucaus.
>
> Prince Tchkarectrile is an intensely respectable individual, anyway, and in all probability would decline to become suddenly rich even if all the franchises of the city were rolled into one and handed him. The Prince does not aspire to more earthly wealth than a few good horses, plenty of firearms of the most modern or ancient make, and a few elaborate suits of clothes of a style that has been in vogue in his country for many centuries. Hunting and fighting is his profession… Like a thoughtful father should, the father of His Highness had this young scion of a numerous nobility learn a trade. The trade selected for him was the one he had worked at, and all his family, when not engaged in warfare with one of the tribes in the next country, that of silver and goldsmith. In his works the Prince has shown wonderful skill. With the crudest imaginable tools he has wrought some of the rarest work in precious metals. His swords and revolvers, the latter of the latest Smith & Wesson design, are inlaid with gold and silver, which, with the workmanship, are valued at a king's ransom almost. Even the buckles that attach his belt about his slender person are of silver, inlaid with fine Arabian gold worth several hundred dollars.

16. Prince Luka

Luka Chkhartishvili.

After the meeting, Prince Luka and his men began to play dice on the floor of the tent. "Princes are but human, after all," concluded the reporter.

Another well-known Georgian rider, Veliko Kvitaishvili, recalled, "When I was 13, there was a lively, animated, sparkling guy, a goldsmith's apprentice. His name was Luka Chkhartishvili. He adored horses and spent most of his free time galloping them in the field. Even back then,

Georgian Trick Riders in American Wild West Shows

Standing on horseback: Luka Chkhartishvili.

he was considered the best rider in the village of Lanchkhuti." According to another rider, Lazare Jorbenadze, just before another trip to America, Luka organized a training field in front of his house where 10 riders could exercise every day.

While on the subject, it's worth mentioning that Luka Chkhartishvili's house was the scene of outlaw and terrorist Erasti Jorbenadze's death on July 10, 1910. Seven police squad officers, including its chief, pinned down, in Luka's house, three terrorists—Metekhi prison (located in Tbilisi) runaway Erasti Jorbenadze, Iliko Imerlishvili, and an unidentified person—demanding their surrender. The shootout lasted for two hours, during which the terrorists killed police officer Shapatava. There was one wounded woman in the house as well as one dead horse and one wounded horse. The roof of the house was badly pockmarked with bullet holes.

After a while the criminals dashed out of the house. Imerlishvili and the unidentified man managed to escape from the police. Jorbenadze was unlucky. He was hiding behind a fence when a local merchant, Kolia Reshetnikoff, noticed him. Jorbenadze immediately killed Reshetnikoff and then committed suicide. Bullet holes on the well and in photos of the house can still be seen even today. On that Sunday, Luka Chkhartishvili was performing with other Georgian riders in the Miller Brothers' show in Long Branch, New Jersey.

16. Prince Luka

Erasti Jorbenadze, left, and Iliko Imerlishvili.

The New York Daily Tribune (April 14, 1901) wrote,

The wonderful horsemanship of Prince Loucca has made him one of the attractions of the show. The Prince comes from Batoum [Batumi], which is two and a half miles from Odessa [sic], and joined the show nine years ago.

Georgian Trick Riders in American Wild West Shows

The Prince is said to have got his title from his fellow countrymen just as the Indian chiefs get their titles from their tribes. Where he comes from he is called the Hetman, meaning headman. He is not of the royal blood and, as Russia is well supplied with princes, it is not expected that the title will be envied. There is not a prouder man connected with the show than he, and one of his esteemed friends is Black Fox, the head Indian chief. An accident happened three years ago, which has cost him grief since. While standing upright on the horse the animal stumbled and broke its neck.

Before that, on August 15, 1896, the *Saturday Times* of South Bend, Indiana, reported that Luka had a near-death experience in Indiana:

The next to get a terrible fall was one of the wild riding Cossacks and he painfully moved from the scene of his mishap, and did not again appear. There were several minor accidents of the same nature, but the climax was reached when Luka, the chief rider of the Cossacks, a central figure at the World's Fair exhibition, and one of the best riders in the world started at a

Group of Georgians, circa 1899.

16. Prince Luka

mad pace along the east side of the arena at a place where the ground was supposed to be solid. He was mounted on the best horse in the outfit—a splendid animal that he had been riding at Chicago during the World's Fair and ever since, and a horse as intelligent and docile as the equine family affords. Suddenly near the northeast corner the swift running animal lurched and then fell headlong forward, his brave rider underneath. A groan of sympathy went up from the audience which but a moment before had been wildly applauding the rider. Both lay motionless and not a sound came from them. People as well as employees rushed to their aid and nearly two minutes were required before the horse was pulled from his rider, which he nearly completely covered and had entangled in the stirrups. The plight of the two had been observed by Mr. Cody himself who came from his dressing room only partly dressed to look mournfully upon the gallant steed, which was found to have broken its neck. Luka was picked up unconscious by his fellow Cossacks, and taken to the dressing room. Nearly everyone thought that he was dead, but when a *Times* representative, and Chief Cassidy, visited the dressing room a few minutes later, he was found to have recovered consciousness and was receiving necessary attention, being able to stand up. He is simply a mass of bone and muscle and in the best condition or it would have killed him. No ordinary man would have lived through it.

Presumably it was this incident described by the unknown rider in his diary:

We were watching Luka's great riding. He was riding with one leg thrown over the saddle, the other in the stirrup, and his body straight out from the body of the horse and parallel to the ground. In rounding the turn the horse slipped and horse and rider went to the ground. Luka lay still and poor horse broke the neck and died. We got scared to death, we thought Luka would not survive! Thanks to God everything worked out.

One member of the audience, an old sailor, told the journalist, "Well, that is indeed wonderful! I've been all over the seas, but I never saw anything like that before! It would be almost impossible for an experienced sailor, no matter how much he knew about barbering, to try to shave himself on a stormy sea without getting cut, but I do believe that the prince could shave himself with as much ease while riding on that horse as one could sitting in a comfortable chair at home." The *Brooklyn Citizen* (July 4, 1894) wrote: "The Prince gives an exhibition of his own skill that seems to take the breath of everybody from them. One of his feats is to work his horse into a full gallop and seemingly dash directly upon the audience, and then when within a distance of a foot from the grandstand pull his horse upon its haunches, he still standing erect upon its back. The horse is then allowed to gently drop upon all fours and dash off in another direction, while its rider gracefully slips into his place in the saddle."¹

According to an article in *Tsnobis Purtsely* dated December 21, 1897, "Mr. Chkhartishvili received a gold medal for his riding skills inscribed with the words: "To Russia's famous player from American society." Other newspapers wrote, "The twelve Cossacks are in charge of Prince Lukka, a man of royal blood, and who, while he cannot speak much English, is as polite as a Chesterfield."² (Lord Philip Dormer Stanhope Chesterfield was an author and intellectual. His book *Letters to His Son* became a bible for the manners of proper English gentlemen.)

> Their leader, Prince Luka, distinguished from his band by a costume of snowy four, rode with all the abandon of a madman, hanging to his fiery steed by the point of his small boot, as the mettlesome little beast tore around the arena at breakneck speed. Then swinging into his lofty saddle he stood erect and swung his heavy, gleaming sword as easily as if it were a diminutive pen knife.
>
> After the show Luka turned out to be a mild-mannered and charmingly pleasant gentleman, who spoke in softest tones of his "papa" and "mamma," his "sweet little sister," and his "happy home" in faraway Russia as tenderly as one could imagine, and then Prince Luka flashed fire from his great dark eyes when questioned as to his opinion of other riders in the show, making answer: "If Lukas thought that any other man-cowboy, soldier or Indian could ride so well as he, Lukas would leave Buffalo Bill and go back to Russia."³

Prince Luka's fame spread throughout all Wild West shows and circuses, and even after his retirement, many performers adopted his name and pretended to be him. Here is a passage from the article published in *Frontier Times Magazine* (Winter 1961):

> Protesting wails emitted from the wagon occupied by Prince Lucka, leader of the Russian Cossacks, and his wife. But the protests from the newborn infant did not stay the routine of Buffalo Bill's Wild West Show. Six-Shooter Junction [now Hempstead, Texas] expected a show, and a minor thing like the birth of an infant boy certainly would not interfere with or delay Six-Shooter Junction's entertainment.
>
> "Buffalo Bill" Cody stopped by the wagon a little later, congratulated John Kischko ("Prince Lucka" of the Cossacks), inquired briefly about the health of mother and child and strode on down the line, checking on the routine of setting up the show.
>
> When he was four, his mother died on the road with the Buffalo Bill Show. When he was eleven, his father was killed during a performance at Chicago,

16. Prince Luka

leaving Glenn to grow up with the show, where he already was a regular hand. His uncle, also a Cossack, called Prince Tifto [possibly Prince Tepho—Teophane Kavtaradze], was with Buffalo Bill, but there had been differences between the Cossack brothers and the uncle felt only a light sense of obligation toward the orphan.[4]

It must be noted that new performers adopted not only Luka's name; when real Russian Cossacks appeared in the Wild West show arenas, they borrowed even the Gurian national clothes—chakura and kabalakhi, which original Cossacks never wore.

Here's another interesting quote from Fred Gipson's book, which the author dedicated to Zack Miller, one of the owners of the Millers Brothers' 101 Ranch, where Luka Chkhartishvili worked from 1908–1914. "They were all packed, and Zack was in their quarters talking to them when in walked some British officers with orders to put the Cossacks on a boat going to Belgium. From there, they would go into Russia and eventually into the war. Lucca, the head of Cossacks, broke down and cried like a kid." Zack tried to console him. "When this is over," he said, "I'll still have a place for you boys." But Lucca shook his head. "For us, sir," he said, "it is all over now. We shall never see the 101 again." This conversation took place in London in August 1914 after the beginning of World War I. The Miller Brothers never knew what became of Lucca and his Cossack riders. For that reason, most books report that the gallant horsemen probably died on the battlefields of Europe during World War. But Luka never fought the war. He stayed home and wanted to emigrate from Georgia to America. He attempted unsuccessfully for years to apply for a visa to return, but never managed to get back to the United States. At home Luka used a cane to walk, since his knees gave out. Usually he was sitting under his pear tree at a table and telling stories of his adventures in America. Luka Chkhartishvili died circa 1936 in Lanchkhuti and was buried in the cemetery of his home town of Gvimbalauri.

17. The Georgian Amazons

The Wild West show's female employees brought more grace to the Georgians' performances. Gurian ladies were also much admired—perhaps as descendants of the original female warrior tribe. Catholic missionary Paul Maria Faianzelli said of them, "They can ride, they can hunt and they usually do it with bow and falcon. It's not hard to believe that they are real Amazons for they ride like men and can handle all kinds of weapons quite well."

As mentioned above, the first Gurian woman who made it to America was Frida Mgaloblishvili; she arrived in 1893. The following year she was performing alongside such star riders such as Dimitri Mgaloblishvili, Vasil Ckhonia, David Ckhonia, and Zosime Pataraia. Very little is known about Frida. She was born on August 7, 1871, in Ozurgeti. As it turned out, Mgaloblishvili was not her real surname. It was Dolidze, and she was a stepsister of Dimitri Mgaloblishvili, despite the fact that they were referred to as a couple in the Wild West show programs.

The World (March 21, 1894) wrote about them: "Very few of them [Cossacks] could speak English, but one, the princess Frieda Dimitri, has been in America before. Her husband's front name is very like a sneeze, and he can shoot champagne corks out of bottles with or without a gun."

Frida's parents were Maka and Simon Dolidzes from Ozurgeti. Frida's father died in her youth, leaving her mother with four children. Maka married Giorgi Mgaloblishvili, a wealthy widower living in the village Onchiketi and the father of Dimitri. Maka left her three sons with the family of Dolidze and took her daughter, Frida, to Onchiketi. Giorgi, one of the area's best riders, loved his horses. Dimitri and Frida learned the skill of riding from their father in the mountains of Guria.[1] One reporter wrote about her: "From her infancy the horse was her plaything and comrade. To ride was her chief amusement and the long journeys of many days' duration, together with wild dashes over the steppes, gave her the wonderful physique that is one of her greatest attractions today."[2]

Giorgi wanted his stepdaughter to receive an education.

> A little needlework, the piano and mandolin were taught by various instructors, and when but twelve years of age the youthful Princess left the odd little province bordering on the Black sea, and went to Paris to be educated as befitted her rank, but as she quaintly observes: "I preferred the riding all the time."[3] Giorgi's brother Ilarion, a priest, had sent his children to a monastery in France for their education. Giorgi took Frida to France and left her in the monastery. After reuniting in France, Dimitri and Frida rode together for two years in American Wild West shows.
>
> The Cossacks are bona fide Cossacks and not Polish Jews with long coats on as they seem. They are from near the Caucasian mountains near the Black Sea. The men cannot speak any English, except to say, whenever you address them on any subject from religion to free silver, "Oh, yes, it's warm in Russia." They are in the charge of a local chief, who is called a prince in the local official directory, and the other Cossacks are afraid of him. They throw salaams at him and he makes them sit at another table when he eats. He is accompanied by the Princess Dimitri. She can talk English, French, and Spanish. She says, and probably truthfully, that she had an English governess as a child. She and her husband and the other Cossacks wear their native dress behind the curtain. Her dress is peculiar and striking. Beginning at the feet she is dressed in high topped boots, baggy plaid trousers of an oriental cut, a tan coat—after the blazer style—fastened with cords in front and covering a silk blouse waist made full in front. It is not a startling costume. The Princess wears it very modestly and does not appear to regret that the contract with the Prince requires that all the Cossacks shall wear their national dress at all times. She says that she likes circus life because all the people about the show are so kind and thoughtful of her.[4]

But not always. On one occasion a member of the audience impudently accosted her. "A Negro insulted Frida Mgaloblishvili, but was promptly and effectually chastised by Dimitri Mgaloblishvili who tapped him on the head with a riding whip, felling the Negro to the ground like an ox."[5]

Sometimes the Wild West performers were not welcomed. According to *The Minneapolis Times* (August 14, 1893):

> The Cossacks connected with the Forepaugh show were denied hospitality in a Minneapolis hotel yesterday, for the only time since they landed in this country last spring. Manager Hoopes, of the National Hotel, made a contract to keep some of the circus people over Sunday. The agent of the show wrote

Georgian Trick Riders in American Wild West Shows

upon the register, Prince Dimitri and princess and six other Cossack names of a more formidable appearance and sound. Manager Hoopes made no objection to the entries, thinking, perhaps, that the Cossacks were ordinary United States mortals when not on view under canvas. Yesterday after the arrival of the circus trains the Cossacks proceeded to the hotel, led by the princess, who is an accomplished linguist, speaking seven or eight languages, and therefore acts as interpreter. The hotel man then discovered that they wore the costumes of their native land, and he didn't like it. He waved his hand in a gesture of repulsion, and exclaimed that the men couldn't stop in his house. He even refused to admit them to the dining room for breakfast.

These Cossacks are proud fellows, as they are all of the noble blood and high standing at home, and though they couldn't understand the language, they did comprehend the gesture. Hungry and chagrined, they precede to the circus grounds and laid their grievances, the princess acting as spokesman, before Manager McCaddon. Manager Hoopes arrived about the same time, and there was a somewhat animated conversation.

"You don't have to take these men if you don't want to," said Mr. McCaddon. "There are plenty of good hotels that will. The Astor house, in New York, and the Continental hotel, in Philadelphia, made no objection to them, and I don't think your hotel is any better."

"I would take them if they wore American costumes," said Mr. Hoopes.

"That is just what they cannot do," said Mr. McCaddon. "Their contract with me compels them to wear their national dresses."

"Will you promise that they will not leave their room?"

"No. If they go to your house they must have the right to do as other guests. These men are much above the average of our foreign population in character, and I would not insult them by such a stipulation as you ask."

Then Hoopes said he didn't want them, and Mr. McCaddon told him if he refused to keep them he must refuse the others on his circus contract, as it was all or none. Hotel agent Abbot was immediately dispatched to transfer all the circus employees to the Hotel Brunswick.

What apparently troubled the Cossacks most about the whole difficulty was that it prevented them from attending church. They are devout members of the Greek Church, and never lose an opportunity to attend service, usually going to the Catholic Church.

On April 1, 1894, *The Morning Journal* ran an interview with Frida Mgaloblishvili. According to the interviewer, Frida, "a genuine lady," had been sent to Paris, where she had collected a perfect command of French, German, Italian, and English.

The following is a shortened version of this interview:

Riding may almost be said to be born with us. Far back as I can remember, the back of a horse was my chair, almost my cradle. I have never learned

17. The Georgian Amazons

Veliko Kvitaishvili and his horsemen on parade, unidentified town, United States, 1912.

riding, never been taught it as most performers are. All the fancy riding I do I did as a child for pure fun in emulation and rivalry of others in my native land. We Cossack women, though we do not vote and practice law or medicine, are born to a greater degree of freedom than your American ladies.... The women in my country, too, have all the material habits of men. They smoke about as much, the delicate, light tobacco grown in our valleys or imported Turkish. They drink with equal freedom the light, bright wines of the Caucasus. Being wine, no spirit drinkers, unlike the Russians, we are an extremely sober people. Drunkenness is almost unknown among us.... Possibly our climate has something to do with the harmony that reigns among us. Possibly our open-air life contributes to this end by making us healthier. Well, our region doesn't oppress us. We are of the Greek Church, and, like the Catholics, we have many holy days, which are holidays. Suppose you visit the Caucasus, you need no letters of introduction. You are invited to stay in the best houses as long as you please, and everything in the house is at your disposal.... We live chiefly by agriculture and hunting. In my girlhood, I have seen wild animals shot from my bedroom window. Our chief drink, next to wine, is tea.... Our people are hearty eaters, but fatness is rare. The men, though slender, are stronger than any I have yet seen.... Our dancing is peculiar. I can not describe it to you.... One of the things that very greatly pleases the spectators is our shooting, when standing on horseback.

Georgian Trick Riders in American Wild West Shows

According to the press, Frida used to perform, with one or four horses Roman riding. Roman riding is one of the older forms of riding and was performed during the time of the Roman Empire. Frida, standing on the backs of two galloping horses, would go around the ring just as hard and fast as they could to the cheers and yelps of an audience. "Brilliant and Dashing Double Four Horse Tandem Hurdle Race, in which the daring originators ride one thoroughbred and rein three others in the lead driven at breakneck speed around the track and leaping high hurdles as they fly. Madame Castrioni & Madame Dimitri."[6] Standing on two bareback horses at full gallop is very difficult, on three horses is uncommon, and on four horses is very rare.

Those who witnessed her breathtaking performance at Madison Square Garden could easily say that she was born a rough rider, a

Clockwise from left: Kirile Pirtskhalaishvili, Kitilia Kvitaishvili, Christephore Imnadze, Veliko Kvitaishvili, Varden Kvitaishvili, Barbale Imnadze, Maro Kvitaishvili.

natural-born horsewoman. Once "Frida Mgaloblishvili was thrown from her horse and quite badly hurt during the evening performance." One week later she "made her first reappearance after her accident."[7]

Frida Mgaloblishvili performed for only two years, afterwards never returning to America and dropping out of view. Stepbrother Dimitri came back each year until 1900.

The Zakareishvili Sisters, Maro and Barbale (Barbara), began to ride in their native Surebi at an early age. The sisters were brave, joyful, and hard-working; they lived life to the fullest. Maro and Barbale were introduced to the public by Luka Chkhartishvili, who hoped to increase interest in the "Cossacks," because their performance was no longer the headlining act. Here is interesting individual information about the riders:

Veliko Kvitaishvili, age 36, can read and write.
Maro Kvitaishvili, wife of Veliko, age 22, can read/write.
Joseph Imnadze, age 36, cannot read or write.
Teimuraz Chkhartishvili, age 37, can read/write.
Joseph Mshvidobadze, age 36, can read/write, 1903/1905, height 5.7, hair grey, eyes brown.
Bartlome Baramidze, age 33, can read/write, 1904/1909, height 5.9, hair black, eyes brown.
Karaman Imnadze, age 35, cannot read or write, 1900/1903.
Konstantine Chkhartishvili, age 40, can read/write, 1905/1908, height 5.7, hair black, eyes brown.
Khalampri Pataraia, age 34, can read/write, 1906/1908, height 5.8, hair black, eyes blue.
Sergia Jorbenadze, age 35, can read/write, 1905/1908, height 5.6, hair black, eyes brown.
Christine Tsintsadze, female, age 36, can read/write, height 5.0, hair black, eyes brown.
Luka Chkhartishvili, age 42, can read/write, 1904/1909, height 5.2, hair black, eyes brown.
Ilarion Ebralidze, age 31, can read/write, 1904/1907, height 5.8, hair blond, eyes blue.
Ilarion Tsintsadze, age 40, cannot read or write, 1901/1904, blind left eye, hair grey.[8]

Georgian Trick Riders in American Wild West Shows

Left to right: **Kitilia Kvitaishvili, Varden Kvitaishvili, Barbale Imnadze, Kirile Tsintsadze, Veliko Kvitaishvili, circa 1912.**

In a letter to Amiran Tsamtsishvili, Ms. Barbale Zakareishvili gives a brief account of her life.

> I'm from poor family from Sajavakho. My father's name is Spiridon. My mother's name is Phedosi. When I turned eight I moved to Lanckhuti with my elder sister. I went to the States when I turned sixteen thanks to my sister and brother in law [Veliko Kvitaishvili]. They had gone three years earlier and invited me to join them. I arrived to America in 1912. They found me a job so that we were all performing at Ringling Brothers' shows. There were seven men and two ladies all in all. But then due to the war the show was closed down. In 1918 I went to Chicago with Veliko Kvitaishvili and several other Georgians. Most of them are dead now. Only two have survived— Kaisar Kvitaishvili, who is 88 now, and Vaso Tsuladze. He's 80. In 1920, my brother-in-law returned to Georgia. I decided to settle in Chicago, got married to Christephore Imnadze [Emnadze] and had four daughters. They are all married now. My husband was alive when they got married and died six months later.

17. The Georgian Amazons

Once in the United States, however, she joined the Georgians and was soon taking part in riding stunts. One of the highlights of Barbale's set was when she rode with the American flag in her hands while standing on the shoulders of two galloping riders. Balance, coordination,

Barbale Imnadze, Chicago, 1985.

physical fitness, and nerve were all prerequisites for doing such tricks. On her way to becoming one of the best female trick riders, Barbale had been thrown, stepped on, and dragged, but injuries never stopped her.

Once Barbale was seriously injured: "The lady Cossack rider had her left collarbone disconnected at the shoulder after leaving the arena in the evening. Her horse tripped while making a leap, and she was thrown against a stake. The bone did not break, but was forced through the ligaments one and one-half inches. The lady left hospital on Friday and with her husband joined the show at Hancock, New York."[9]

Another lady rider, Christine Tsintsadze, was born in the small village of Sujuna. Her maiden name is Nodia. She spent her childhood in Lanckhuti, and in her relatives' words, she often pretended that she had business in neighboring villages just to be able to ride a horse. By and large, Luka Chkhartishvili was responsible for encouraging female riders to go to America. Crossing the Atlantic was a strenuous experience, not to mention exhaustive daily training and performances, but the ladies coped with it like the men did. Christine Tsintsadze's parents were against sending their daughter to a distant country, but she was strongly determined to go, undergoing training at Luka's training fields to prepare herself.

Christine went to America in 1908 with a group of riders that included Maro and Veliko Kvitaishvilis, Teimuraz and Konstantine Chkhartishvilis, Joseph and Kharaman Imnadzes, Bartlome Jorbenadze, Khalampri Pataraia, Ilarion Ebralidze, and Bartlome Mshvidobadze. They went to America via Germany.

The riders split into two groups after arriving in America. The first one stayed with Pawnee Bill's show in New York, and the second (Maro and Veliko Kvitaishvilis, Christine Tsintsadze, Teimuraz Chkhartishvili, Khalampri Pataraia, Luka Chkhartishvili) joined one of the shows in Cincinnati, Ohio.

Christine Tsintsadze was an extremely brave lady. Once, when her horse fell, she hit her head on the ground and lost several teeth but nevertheless managed to finish her set and was awarded fancy clothes, a golden watch, and a ring. All in all, she had three near-death experiences during four years but stubbornly went on performing. It's worth mentioning that her admirers attempted to kidnap her a couple of times but failed, thanks to Christine's Georgian colleagues. Later, Ms. Tsintsadze recalled that nearly all her fans, even the women, tried to kiss her on

17. The Georgian Amazons

Maro and Veliko Kvitaishvilis.

the mouth after performances. "Probably it was my white teeth in perfect shape that they liked," joked Christine.

Christine returned to Georgia in 1912, and the whole town of Lantckhuti turned out to meet her and another group of riders at the station like heroes. She continued performing in Georgia and once even won 1,000 rubles in one race. She became a well-known healer and healed neighbors with folk remedies. Christine collected herbs and made various extracts that facilitated the condition of patients.

On her deathbed, Christine Tsintsadze gave away all her dresses and other personal belongings that she had been presented with in America and, unfortunately, burned a huge box full of private correspondence.

Crowds marveled at Maro Kvitaishvili's ability to circle a horse's belly at full gallop or ride three or four horses simultaneously, often asking her to show them her soles to make sure she had no glue on them. For her outstanding achievements she was presented with a golden ring by one of the show's organizers. *The San Francisco Examiner* (August 31, 1913) reported about the accident that presumably happened to Maro:

Just about the time the industrious workers with the concert tickets were selling their loudest, a Miss Cossack, or maybe it was a Madame Cossack, cossacked too abruptly around a turn, lost her balance and rode half the length of the tent hanging by a toe-nail. Whereupon the band quit playing, the umpty-hundred employees of the Messrs. Ringling betrayed a heap of alarm, the spectators stood up and held their breaths, and the newspaper men got mildly excited in anticipation of a story not down on the schedule. But, the Cossack lady—she belongs to the Wellico Kutoshevly troupe, so perhaps she is Miss Well, etc.—[was] helped out of her predicament by the stage hands, or the ring hands, or the what-you-may-call-em hands, and the sole sufferer was the unfortunate horse, which took a cut across the midsection from the irate rider's whip.

Maro continued to ride until old age, once she had been thrown, and that didn't prevent her from riding.

Veliko Kvitaishvili recalled,

Later, I signed a contract and started to recruit the Georgian riders on my own. Here are the names of some of them: Kirile Pirtskhalaishvili, Barbale Zakareishvili (my wife's sister), Christephore Imnadze, and Kitila Kvitaishvili (my brother). I worked with these riders independently for ten years. The winter season used to open in Chicago. When it got warmer we moved to

Veliko Kvitaishvili's horsemen.

17. The Georgian Amazons

New York and performed at open-air hippodromes. We traveled to many American cities and towns. They had our pictures and posters all over the place. We usually started our performances with parading in the streets with the rest of the performers. We used to open with Georgian songs and dance. The program consisted of 29 acts. Our riders were deliberately put in the last act because we usually took the arenas by storm. As soon as we entered the ring we were deafened by the applause of 12, 000 people.

As mentioned above, Veliko Kvitaishvili brought his wife's sister, Barbale, to America, because his wife gave birth to two children in America, while two older ones were waiting for her in Georgia. Veliko Kvitaishvili returned to Georgia in 1924. Soon after, the Kvitaishvilis wanted to return to the United States, but the Bolsheviks would not let them out of Batumi. Barbale and her husband Christephore Imnadze (Emnadze) stayed in America and continued to perform.

After years working in the Ringling circus, Barbara and Christephore settled in Chicago. Barbara worked at the Kellogg switchboard in Chicago, and Christephore was employed by W. O. Smith at Union Market. They had four daughters: Evelyn, Marie, Florence, and Nina. All of them were married in America. Christopher died October 14, 1953, and is buried in Chicago in a Georgian cemetery. Barbale Imnadze died in 1988 in Chicago. Three years later, the Georgian Soviet Socialist Republic became the independent country of Georgia.

The obituary printed in *Chicago Tribune* (January 20, 1988) said:

Services for Barbara Emnadze, 90, one of the first woman members of the Cossack-style riding troupe of Ringling Brothers and Barnum & Bailey Circus, will be held at 11 a.m. Friday in Holy Trinity Orthodox Cathedral, 1121 N. Leavitt St.

The church is the same one in which Mrs. Emnadze was married in 1920. Mrs. Emnadze, a former resident of Chicago's Canaryville neighborhood, died Saturday in a Spooner, Wisconsin, nursing home.

She was born in Russia's Georgia area and came to the United States in 1912 at age 15 at the request of her sister and brother-in-law, both riders in the circus's Cossack troop.

Mrs. Emnadze's sister, a member of the troop for a short time, had become pregnant and had to retire. Mrs. Emnadze was summoned to the U.S. to take her place, although at the time she had done only the tame horseback riding that was typical of farm girls of the period.

Once in the U.S., however, she joined the Cossack troop and, with the reckless courage of a teenager, was soon taking part in riding stunts such as standing upright on a galloping horse's back and standing on the shoulders

Barbale Imnadze and Veliko Kvitaishvili.

of two male riders waving an American flag as they galloped around the circus ring.

Mrs. Emnadze remained with the circus for six years until the troupe was disbanded during World War I. Then she settled in Chicago, working as a waitress and for Switchboard Company.

17. The Georgian Amazons

While she was with the circus Mrs. Emnadze had met her husband-to-be, Christofor, a onetime Russian army cavalryman who was working as a Cossack-style rider for the rival 101 Ranch Wild West Show and the Buffalo Bill's Wild West Show.

The couple were married in Chicago in 1920. Her husband, who left the Wild West Show business and who died in 1953, worked as a groom caring for the horses of Chicagoans who stabled their mounts on Union Stock Yards grounds.

In 1969, Mrs. Emnadze made a return trip to her home village and received an enthusiastic welcome.

She is survived by four daughters, Evelyn Martinkus, Mary Mazeika, Nina McGleam and Florence Murphy; nine grandchildren and four great-grandchildren.

Presumably there was fifth female rider named Babilina Zascetely (possibly Tsereteli). She rode in three different shows: Jones Brothers show in 1910, California Frank's Wild West in 1911, and in 1913 in Tompkins Wild West show with a man called Archil Zascetely (Tsereteli). Here is an article connected with the accident: "Princess Babilina Zascetely, Lady Cossack, has the misfortune to have her horse fall with

Barbale Imnadze.

her during the evening performance at Carbondale, PA. Before the cowboys could release her the horse kicked her several times, breaking both collar bones and right shoulder-blade." After month and a half the same newspaper announced that "Babilina Zascetely has returned after a six-week confinement at the hospital."[10] But still, there is a very little information about her.

18. This Is the End

World War I and the Bolsheviks ended the Georgians' voyages abroad. Those Georgians who found themselves stuck in the States, mostly in Chicago, continued performing in Miller and Ringling Brothers' circuses and returned to their homeland only when the war was over. Many Georgians settled down to create typical American families and lost ties with their homeland.

According to author Paul Reddin, Cossacks, long a staple in the Wild West shows, enchanted Americans anew in 1920 because of the Bolshevik Revolution in 1917. They were real Russian Cossacks who fled their country when Bolsheviks came to power. Their anticommunism, manliness, colorful costumes, musical ability, and dances appealed to Americans. In addition, many of Miller's compatriots hoped for a softening of communism and improvement in American-Soviet relations. The Millers, however, did not use the Cossacks to discuss the Bolshevik Revolution, Czarist Russia, or relations between the United States and the Soviet Union. In an effort to capitalize on the Cossacks' popularity, the Millers sent them on an off-season tour; they performed a dagger dance and a knife throwing, also roller-skating; however, some ran away, others refused to finish tours, and at times American audiences did not warm to them.[1]

The occasional feeble attempt by some to reanimate the previous glory of the shows led to tasteless endeavors in which some of the Georgian original participants were enlisted. But by that time they had lost the luster of stardom along with their energy and endurance. Fatally, the media had lost interest in them. The organizers even stopped mentioning their names in the programs.

In 1925, Teophane Kavtaradze (Chief Tephon), Khariton Chkonia, Kaisar Kvitaishvili, and one unidentified person were still in the United States working on the Miller Brothers' 101 Ranch show.[2] But fact is that when Georgian left the Wild West shows, there was nobody to fill their boots, even genuine Russian Cossacks who after the 1917 revolution and

Georgian Trick Riders in American Wild West Shows

Kaisar Kvitaishvili (courtesy Buffalo Bill Museum and Grave, Golden, Colorado).

Russian Civil War fled to America. "The Wild West Shows were good in those days," said one old timer, "because the men who made them put their hearts into their work. They spared nothing for realism. The era ended because the old blood died off and the youngsters didn't have the stuff to carry on."[3]

Hard times were ahead for those who returned to Georgia as well. In February 1921, four corps of the Red Army struck simultaneously from five directions. Against this powerful force, Georgia had about 40,000 troops of the Regular Army and National Guard spread over all fronts. During the three years of independence, Georgia didn't get a single gun or a single case of ammunition from the West.

In spite of the extraordinary heroism of the Georgian Army, they were unable to resist the Soviet invasion, especially since Turkey entered the war on the side of Soviet Russia. Thus, by perfidy, treachery, and

18. This Is the End

brute force, Communist Russia brought to an end the independence of Georgia, just as Czarist Russia had done 120 years previously in 1801.[4]

On the grounds that Georgian horsemen all were American spies, most of the riders were imprisoned or exiled by the Bolsheviks. In 1937,

Ivane Baramidze (courtesy Buffalo Bill Museum and Grave, Golden, Colorado).

Ivane Baramidze was captured at the railway station, and his fate is unknown. It is known that Ivane Makharadze had a well tamed horse, and when Bolsheviks came into Georgia and demanded his horse, he refused to give it to them. Instead, Bolsheviks captured Ivane's son and sent him to Siberia. Ivane's grandchild was born there. Ivane Makharadze died in October 1921. He was buried in the churchyard of his village. Soon Bolsheviks ruined the church and destroyed the cemetery. Ivane Makharadze's grave was lost.

Many riders had to destroy all evidence and photographs of their trips abroad in order to survive living in the new regime's iron hands. Often, various random and unrelated titles were given to these photos. One of the photos depicts the Gurians with a cowboy, but the back of the picture says: "Proletarians of all the countries, unite!" This is the political slogan of Karl Marx and Friedrich Engels. Another example is the photo taken in New York, where the Gurians sat in a car with different members of the show. The back of the picture states: "Gurian riders united with local strikers," which of course was not true.

Bolsheviks suppressed all information of Georgians having been in America. Anyone who talked about America and how wonderful it was was called a spy. There were cases when riders were forced to sign a document in which they promised never to mention America or Europe again—a good example is rider Tsintsadze, who, after signing such a document, returned home and died of heart attack.

The Bolsheviks confiscated all the precious gifts and presents they had been given. Usually, these things surfaced in the houses of the party bosses. Daughters of the rider Pavle Makharadze recalled: "They used to take different things that had been brought from the United States from the families of all riders. Finally they took a comb and a tab from our family. My mother was so horrified that she fell ill. She was always waiting for the Bolsheviks to come again." Many horsemen just vanished into the gulags, some committed suicide, and others died in oblivion.

The Georgian riders, so long misnamed, were not out to become famous or make history. They were doing what they did best to make a living and support their loved ones. In Western Europe and the United States they faced unknown languages and alien cultures. But they adapted to the new world quite well, making friends and sometimes families. These trick riders who performed for Buffalo Bill and other

18. This Is the End

Georgian riders, New York, 1908.

American showmen might be viewed as the first Georgian ambassadors to the United States. The connection between Buffalo Bill and Georgian trick riders represents one of the oldest known relationships between Georgia and the United States of America.

Chapter Notes

Introduction

1. http://en.wikipedia.org/wiki/John_Shalikashvili.
2. Anna Geifman, *Thou Shalt Kill: Revolutionary Terrorism in Russia, 1894–1917* (Princeton: Princeton University Press, 1993), p. 256.
3. (a.) Cossack is a Turkic word taken to mean "adventure freebooter," adopted as an ethnic name by Turkic tribal groups of the Eurasian steppes. (b.) A person (especially in Czarist Russia) belonging to any of certain groups of Slavs living chiefly in the Southern part of Russia, and forming an elite corps of horsemen. *Georgian Soviet Encyclopedia, Vol. 5* (Tbilisi: 1980), p. 315.
4. *The Pittsburg Post*, Tuesday, May 18, 1909.
5. *Eau Claire Sunday Leader*, June 17, 1906.
6. http://www.archive.org/stream/aroundblackseaas00curtrich/aroundblackseaas00curtrich_djvu.txt.
7. Ibid.

Chapter 1

1. http://www.kvevri.org/.
2. Simon C. Sidamon-Eristoff, *For My Grandchildren* (NP, 2002), p. 2.
3. Translated from Georgian by Kakha Tolordava.
4. Georgian Historical Sketches, Sabchota Sakaretvelo, Tbilisi, Vol. I, 1970, p. 53.
5. William Edward David Allen, *A History of the Georgian People: From the Beginning Down to the Russian Conquest in the 19th Century* (London: Routledge & Kegan Paul, 1971), p. xii.
6. George and Helen Papashvily, *Anything Can Happen* (New York: Harper & Brothers, 1945), p. 62.

Chapter 2

1. http://www.magticom.ge/magazine/1999-4/1999-4-10.html.
2. Vasily Potto, *Caucasian War*, Vol. 4 (Moscow: Tsentrpoligraf, 2006), p. 283.
3. "Off to Guria," *The World of Constant Connection Magazine* 4, 1999, pp. 37–38.
4. Lady Colin Campbell, "A Woman's Walks," *The World*, London, January 6, 1903.
5. Luigi Villari, *Fire and Sword in the Caucasus* (London: T. F. Unwin, 1906), p. 84. http://armenianhouse.org/villari/caucasus/fire-and-sword.html.

Chapter 3

1. WFC Scrapbook, July 29, 1888, Buffalo Bill Historical Center.
2. Adjara is located in the southwestern corner of Georgia, bordered by Turkey to the south and the eastern end of the Black Sea. Adjara is a home to the Adjar ethnic subgroup of Georgians.
3. *Story of the Great American West* (Pleasantville, NY: Reader's Digest, 1977), p. 244.
4. Ibid., p. 245.
5. http://www.historicalinsights.com/dave/cody.html.
6. Steve Friesen, *Buffalo Bill: Scout, Showman, Visionary* (Golden, CO: Fulcrum, 2010), p. 88.
7. Peter Bogdanovich, *John Ford* (Oakland: University of California Press, 1978), p. 104.
8. http://tonymacklin.net/content.php?cID=220.
9. Richard J. Salsbury and Milton S. Walsh, *The Making of Buffalo Bill: A Study in Heroics* (Indianapolis: Bobbs-Merrill, 1928), p. 293.

10. http://segonku.unl.edu/~brogers/bbww/analysis/congress/cwf.php.
11. http://www.unc.edu/depts/diplomat/item/2011/0912/ca/bridges_georgia.html.
12. Imereti is a region in western Georgia.
13. *The London Daily News*, June 2, 1892.
14. *Defiance Crescent-News*, September 7, 1943.
15. Racha is a part of Georgia, in the mountains northeast of Guria.
16. *Royal Cornwall Gazette*, June 2, 1904.
17. *St. Paul Dispatch*, September 18, 1896.
18. *The Nashville Banner*, October 8, 1897.
19. *The Washington Post*, Monday, April 24, 1893.
20. *Brooklyn Citizen*, July 4, 1894.
21. Richard Alexis Georgian, *Cossacks, Indians and Buffalo Bill: The Adventures of Georgian Riders in America* (Naples, FL: Barringer, 2011), p. 46.
22. *The Washington Post*, Monday, April 24, 1893.
23. *Collier's Weekly*, April 13, 1901.
24. *Tsnobis Purtsely*, June 27, 1897.

Chapter 4

1. *Harper's Weekly*, Vol. XXXVI, No. 1863, Saturday, September 3, 1892.
2. Don Cossacks are from the Donets Basin and Don River north of the Kuban lowland and the North Caucasus Mountains in Russia.
3. Richard J. Salsbury and Milton S. Walsh, *The Making of Buffalo Bill: A Study in Heroics* (Indianapolis: Bobbs-Merrill, 1928), p. 295.
4. *Pen and Pencil*, June 16, 1892.
5. Alan Gallop, *Buffalo Bill's British Wild West* (Gloucestershire: Sutton, 2001), pp. 98–99.
6. Richard J. Salsbury and Milton S. Walsh, *The Making of Buffalo Bill: A Study in Heroics* (Indianapolis: Bobbs-Merrill, 1928), p. 295.
7. *Pen and Pencil*, July 16, 1892.
8. *Omaha Daily Bee*, June 19, 1892.

9. *The Morning*, June 3, 1892.
10. The vast geographical region of Europe and Asia that was controlled by the Mongols in the 13th and 14th centuries. http://www.audioenglish.org/dictionary/tartary.htm.
11. Richard J. Salsbury and Milton S. Walsh, *The Making of Buffalo Bill: A Study in Heroics* (Indianapolis: Bobbs-Merrill, 1928), p. 295.
12. http://query.nytimes.com/gst/abstract.html?res=F40812F8355C12738DDDAE0894DC405B818CF1D3.
13. Larry McMurtry, *The Colonel and Little Missie: Buffalo Bill, Annie Oakley, and the Beginnings of Superstardom in America* (New York: Simon & Schuster, 2006), p. 183.
14. Richard J. Salsbury and Milton S. Walsh, *The Making of Buffalo Bill: A Study in Heroics* (Indianapolis: Bobbs-Merrill, 1928), p. 293.

Chapter 5

1. Alan Gallop, *Buffalo Bill's British Wild West* (Gloucestershire: Sutton, 2001), p. 192.
2. Ibid., p. 192
3. "Exhibited Before Queen Victoria," *Brooklyn Daily Eagle*, Sunday, June 26, 1892.
4. Ibid.
5. Joseph G. Rosa and Robin May, *Buffalo Bill and His Wild West: A Pictorial Biography* (Lawrence: University Press of Kansas, 1989), p 156.
6. Alan Gallop, *Buffalo Bill's British Wild West* (Gloucestershire: Sutton, 2001), pp. 194–195.
7. Nate Salsbury, "The Origin of the Wild West Show," *The Colorado Magazine*, July, 1955, p. 210.
8. Don Russell, *Wild West: A History of the Wild West Shows* (Austin: University of Texas Press, 1970), pp. 41–42.
9. http://www.stgeorges-windsor.org/archives/blog/?tag=buffalo-bill.
10. Nate Salsbury, "The Origin of the Wild West Show," *The Colorado Magazine*, July, 1955, pp. 208–211.
11. Louis S. Warren, *Buffalo Bill's America: William Cody and the Wild West Show* (New York: Vintage Books, 2007), p. 495.

12. Tom F. Cunningham, "*Your Fathers the Ghosts*": *Buffalo Bill's Wild West in Scotland* (Edinburgh: Black & White, 2007), p. 157.

13. Richard Alexis Georgian, *Cossacks, Indians and Buffalo Bill: The Adventures of Georgian Riders in America* (Naples, FL: Barringer, 2011), p. 397.

14. Gurieli was a noble family and a ruling dynasty (dukes) of Guria.

15. *New York Daily Tribune*, Sunday, March 15, 1903.

16. Tom F. Cunningham, "*Your Fathers the Ghosts*": *Buffalo Bill's Wild West in Scotland* (Edinburgh: Black & White, 2007), p. 188.

17. *The Dumfries & Galloway Saturday Standard*, September 3, 1904.

18. *The Pelican*, February 13, 1903.

Chapter 6

1. *Brooklyn Daily Eagle*, April 12, 1897.

2. Tom F. Cunningham, "*Your Fathers the Ghosts*": *Buffalo Bill's Wild West in Scotland* (Edinburgh: Black & White, 2007), p. 158.

3. *Tsnobis Purtsely*, April 16, 1903.

4. Donald Rayfield, *The Literature of Georgia: A History* (London: Routledge, 2000), p. 9.

5. Sarah J. Blackstone, *Buckskins, Bullets, and Business: A History of Buffalo Bill's Wild West* (Westport, CT: Greenwood, 1986), p. 83.

6. http://www.historicalinsights.com/dave/cody.html.

7. *Star*, May 31, 1892.

8. *Saturday Review*, July 2, 1892.

9. Winnipeg Theatre Listings, June 16–21, 1913.

10. Richard Alexis Georgian, *Cossacks, Indians and Buffalo Bill: The Adventures of Georgian Riders in America* (Naples, FL: Barringer, 2011), p. 32.

11. Imam Shamil (1797–1871)—political and religious leader of the Muslim tribes of the Northern Caucasus.

12. http://segonku.unl.edu/~brogers/bbww/documents/1893program.php.

13. "Buffalo Bill Has Drawn on Many Lands," *The Daily Picayune*, New Orleans, November 2, 1902.

14. *St. Louis Star*, May 7, 1907.

15. Louis S. Warren, *Buffalo Bill's America: William Cody and the Wild West Show* (New York: Vintage Books, 2007), p. 424.

16. http://www.ushmm.org/wlc/en/article.php?ModuleId=10005183.

17. http://www.circushistory.org/Bandwagon/bw-1963Nov.htm.

Chapter 7

1. *Washtenaw Times*, July 13, 1900.

2. http://www.sandiegohistory.org/journal/60july/cody.htm.

3. *American Cowboy*, Buffalo Bill, Collector's Edition, 2012–2013.

4. *Tsnobis Purtsely*, April 16, 1903.

5. http://query.nytimes.com/gst/abstract.html?res=F40812F8355C12738DDDAE0894DC405B818CF1D3.

6. Joy S. Kasson, *Buffalo Bill's Wild West: Celebrity, Memory, and Popular History* (New York: Hill and Wang, 2001), p. 5.

7. Sandra K. Sagala, Buffalo Bill on Stage (Albuquerque: University of New Mexico Press, 2008), p. 203.

8. *Frontier Times Magazine*, Winter 1961.

9. Ibid.

10. Thomas M. Barrett, "All the World's a Frontier: How Cossacks Became Cowboys," *Humanities*, Volume 22, No. 3, January/February 2001. http://www.neh.gov/humanities/2001/januaryfebruary/feature/all-the-worlds-frontier.

11. Colonel William F. Cody, Colonel Prentiss Ingraham, Helen Cody Wetmore, and Elmer Sherwood, *The Buffalo Bill Megapeck: 5 Classic Books About Buffalo Bill Cody* (Rockville, MD: Wildside Press, 2013), p. 540.

12. http://www.eyewitnesstohistory.com/buffalobill.htmIn.

13. George and Helen Papashvily, *Anything Can Happen* (New York: Harper & Brothers, 1945), pp. 4–6.

14. Jon E. Lewis, The Mammoth Book of the West (New York: Carroll & Graf Publishers, 1996).

15. Michelle Delaney, Buffalo Bill's Wild

West Warriors: A Photographic History by Geretrude Kasebier, (Washington, D.C.: Smithsonian Books, 2007), p. 23.

16. Vladimir Gilyarovsky, *Moscow and Muscovites*, Volume 3 (Moscow, 1989), pp. 168–169.

17. Sandra K. Sagala, Buffalo Bill on Stage (Albuquerque: University of New Mexico Press, 2008), p. 203.

18. Steve Friesen, *Buffalo Bill: Scout, Showman, Visionary* (Golden, CO: Fulcrum, 2010), p. 98.

19. Michelle Delaney, Buffalo Bill's Wild West Warriors: A Photographic History by Geretrude Kasebier, (Washington, D.C.: Smithsonian Books, 2007), p. 23.

20. Jane Tompkins, *West of Everything: The Inner Life of Westerns* (Oxford: Oxford University Press, 1992), p. 196.

21. Janet Walker, editor, *Westerns: Films Through History* (London: Routledge, 2001), p. 125.

22. Jim Kitses and Gregg Rickman, editors, *The Western Reader* (Pompton Plains, NJ: Limelight Editions, 2004), pp. 87–88.

23. Jon E. Lewis, *The Mammoth Book of the West* (New York: Carroll & Graf Publishers, 1996), p. 498.

24. Richard J. Salsbury and Milton S. Walsh, *The Making of Buffalo Bill: A Study in Heroics* (Indianapolis: Bobbs-Merrill, 1928), p. 359.

25. Sandra K. Sagala, Buffalo Bill on Stage (Albuquerque: University of New Mexico Press, 2008), p. 204.

26. http://www.montecitojournal.net/archive/14/16/1443/.

27. Chief Red Fox, *The Memoirs of Chief Red Fox* (New York: McGraw-Hill, 1971), p. 103.

Chapter 8

1. The "Wolf Ticket" was a serious impediment to one's career. The "Wolf Ticket" blacklisted the "owner" from work and restricted movements to his village or town. He/she was forbidden to continue seminary studies or to hold a job.

2. *Washington Post*, July 1, 1902.

3. G. Khachapurudze and Noe Jordania, Czarist "Okhranka" Archive Documents (Tbilisi, State Publishing, 1931), p. 46.

Chapter 9

1. Adam Forepaugh (1831–1890), American businessman and circus owner.

2. Eristavi in Georgian means "head of the people." In the Georgian aristocratic hierarchy, it was the title of the third rank of prince and governor of a large province.

3. *New York Daily Tribune*, Thursday, March 30, 1893.

4. *The New York Times*, Friday, March 31, 1893

5. Alexandre Tarsaidze, *Czars and Presidents: The Story of a Forgotten Friendship* (New York: Mcdowell, 1958), p. 185.

6. *Topeka State Journal*, August 29, 1893.

7. George and Helen Papashvily, *Anything Can Happen* (New York: Harper & Brothers, 1945), p. 1.

8. Simon C. Sidamon-Eristoff, *For My Grandchildren* (NP, 2002), p. 218.

9. Richard Alexis Georgian, *Cossacks, Indians and Buffalo Bill: The Adventures of Georgian Riders in America* (Naples, FL: Barringer, 2011), p. 59.

10. Ibid., p. 61

11. Erik Larson, *The Devil in the White City* (New York: Crown, 2003), p. 207.

12. R. L. Wilson and Greg Martin, *Buffalo Bill's Wild West: An American Legend* (New York: Random House, 1998), p. 162.

13. Steve Friesen, *Buffalo Bill: Scout, Showman, Visionary* (Golden, CO: Fulcrum, 2010), p. 90.

14. R. L. Wilson and Greg Martin, *Buffalo Bill's Wild West: An American Legend* (New York: Random House, 1998), p. 162.

15. *The Oracle*, May 28, 1892.

16. *Wisconsin State Journal*, July 24, 1901.

17. *Tsnobis Purtsely*, April 16, 1903.

Chapter 10

1. *The Herald*, July 28, 1897.

2. Nino Nakashidze, *Selected Works*, Volume I (Tbilisi, 1960), p. 293.

3. *The Herald*, July 23, 1897.

Chapter Notes

4. Richard Alexis Georgian, *Cossacks, Indians and Buffalo Bill: The Adventures of Georgian Riders in America* (Naples, FL: Barringer, 2011), pp. 362–363.
5. Ibid., p. 19.
6. Sarah J. Blackstone, *Buckskins, Bullets, and Business: A History of Buffalo Bill's Wild West* (Westport, CT: Greenwood, 1986), p. 79.
7. *Louisiana Missouri Press*, September 27, 1900.
8. *Minneapolis Tribune*, August 13, 1900.
9. Richard Alexis Georgian, *Cossacks, Indians and Buffalo Bill: The Adventures of Georgian Riders in America* (Naples, FL: Barringer, 2011), p. 345.
10. Tevdore Glonti, "A Review of the Current Economic Conditions in Guria," *Akhali Gza* (*New Path*), July 9, 1910.
11. *Greensboro Daily News*, December 30, 1923.
12. *New York Dramatic Mirror*, July 29, 1893.
13. *The New York Times*, Wednesday, May 10, 1905.
14. *New York Clipper*, June 24, 1893.

Chapter 11

1. Richard Alexis Georgian, *Cossacks, Indians and Buffalo Bill: The Adventures of Georgian Riders in America* (Naples, FL: Barringer, 2011), p. 72.
2. *The New York Daily Tribune*, April 14, 1901.
3. *Pen and Pencil*, July 16, 1892.
4. http://www.archive.org/stream/aroundblackseaas00curtrich/aroundblackseaas00curtrich_djvu.txt.
5. Simon C. Sidamon-Eristoff, *For My Grandchildren* (NP, 2002), p. 248.
6. *Tsnobis Purtsely*, June 27, 1897.
7. *Kansas City Times*, September 13, 1909.
8. *Chicago Evening Post*, June 6, 1896.
9. *Daily News-Tribune*, Muscatine, Iowa, October 3, 1896.
10. *Chicago Evening Post*, June 6, 1896.
11. Buffalo Bill Historical Center, William F. Cody Collection, MS 6, Series VI G, Box 3, folder 10.
12. *State Journal*, Lincoln, NE, Sunday, September 18, 1910.
13. Sarah J. Blackstone, *Buckskins, Bullets, and Business: A History of Buffalo Bill's Wild West* (Westport, CT: Greenwood, 1986), p. 82.
14. Nino Nakashidze, *Selected Works*, Volume I (Tbilisi, 1960), p. 296.
15. *Pen and Pencil*, July 16, 1892.
16. Buffalo Bill Historical Center, August 31, 1901.
17. Frank E. Dean, *Complete Book of Trick and Fancy Riding* (Caldwell, ID: Caxton, 1974), p.118.
18. *Hamilton Spectator*, Hamilton, Ontario, July 17, 1897.
19. http://codyarchive.org/memorabilia/wfc.eph00007.html.
20. http://www.winnipegrealestatenews.com/Resources/Article/?sysid=1695.
21. http://www.theswanseabay.co.uk/articles/4/Lifestyle-Leisure/58/BuffaloBillComestoTown!.html.
22. *San Francisco Call*, Volume 87, Number 92, 31 August 1902.
23. *The Hartford Daily Courant*, Saturday, May 28, 1898.
24. *The Washington Post*, Tuesday, May 8, 1898.
25. Richard J. Salsbury and Milton S. Walsh, *The Making of Buffalo Bill: A Study in Heroics* (Indianapolis: Bobbs-Merrill, 1928), p. 293.
26. *City Press*, England, June 22, 1892.
27. *The Washington Post*, April 25, 1893.
28. Frank E. Dean, *Complete Book of Trick and Fancy Riding* (Caldwell, ID: Caxton \, 1974), pp. 219–220.
29. *New York Daily Tribune*, July 22.
30. Frank E. Dean, *Complete Book of Trick and Fancy Riding* (Caldwell, ID: Caxton, 1974), p. 66.
31. Ibid., p. 2.
32. *The Philadelphia Inquirer*, April 9, 1894.
33. *Boston Globe*, June 16, 1907.
34. *The Evening News*, Toronto, Canada, Tuesday, July 6, 1897.
35. *The Philadelphia Press*, May 23, 1904.
36. *Nashville American*, October 7, 1897.
37. *Billboard*, July 28, 1906.

38. Ellsworth Collings and Alma Miller England, *The 101 Ranch* (Norman: University of Oklahoma Press, 1971), p. 170.
39. *San Francisco Chronicle*, October 11, 1908.
40. *The Washington Post*, Monday, April 24, 1893.
41. "Pawnee Bill's Historic Wild West and Great Far East," http://blogs.baylor.edu/texascollection/2011/05/24/pawnee-bills-historic-wild-west-and-great-far-east/.
42. Bailey C. Hanes, *Bill Pickett, Bulldogger (Biography of a Black Cowboy)* (Norman: University of Oklahoma Press, 1989), p. 118.
43. Richard J. Salsbury and Milton S. Walsh, *The Making of Buffalo Bill: A Study in Heroics* (Indianapolis: Bobbs-Merrill, 1928), p. 296.
44. Dee Brown, *The American West* (New York: Scribner, 1994), p. 388.
45. Bob Wade, *Cowgirls* (Layton, UT: Gibbs Smith, 1995).
46. *The Syracuse Herald*, Tuesday, February 14, 1911.
47. Frank E. Dean, *Complete Book of Trick and Fancy Riding* (Caldwell, ID: Caxton, 1974), pp. 2–3.
48. Richard C. Rattenbury, *Arena Legacy: The Heritage of American Rodeo* (Norman: University of Oklahoma Press, 2010), p. 10.

Chapter 12

1. Giorgi Dolidze, *Georgian Film—Past and Present* (Tbilisi, 1985), pp. 43–44.
2. http://www.harrimaninstitute.org/MEDIA/01773.pdf.
3. *Sovetsky Ekran*, 1926 #3, pp. 4–5.

Chapter 13

1. http://frontiers.loc.gov/intldl/mtfhtml/mfpercep/perceprusso.html.
2. Tarsaidze, Alexandre Tarsaidze, *Czars and Presidents: The Story of a Forgotten Friendship* (New York: Mcdowell, 1958), p. 334.
3. http://www.jcs-group.com/johnwayne/wildwest/greatest.html.
4. *The Daily Republican*, Phoenixville, PA, May 23, 1904, p. 1.
5. *The Daily Times*, Oklahoma City, April 20, 1904.
6. *Newcastle Guardian*, Saturday, April 23, 1904, p. 6.
7. *The Sioux City Journal*, Thursday, May 19, 1904.
8. Ernest Poole, *The Bridge: My Own Story* (New York, MacMillan, 1940), p. 160.
9. http://armenianhouse.org/villari/caucasus/gurian-republic.html.
10. Stephen F. Jones, Socialism in Georgian Colors: The European Road to Social Democracy 1883–1917 (Cambridge, MA: Harvard University Press, 2005), p. 156.

Chapter 14

1. *Tsnobis Purtsely*, April 12, 1903.
2. *Hamilton Spectator*, Ontario, July 17, 1897.
3. *The Sioux City Daily Tribune*, May 19, 1904.
4. Richard J. Salsbury and Milton S. Walsh, *The Making of Buffalo Bill: A Study in Heroics* (Indianapolis: Bobbs-Merrill, 1928), p. 295.
5. Jill Jonnes, *Eiffel's Tower: And the World's Fair Where Buffalo Bill Beguiled Paris, the Artists Quarreled, and Thomas Edison Became a Count* (New York: Viking Club, 2009), p. 284.
6. *Austin Daily Herald*, June 22, 1905.
7. *The Herald*, July 28, 1897.
8. Bobby Bridger, *Buffalo Bill and Sitting Bull: Inventing the Wild West* (Austin: University of Texas Press, 2002), p. 311.
9. Alan Gallop, *Buffalo Bill's British Wild West* (Gloucestershire: Sutton, 2001), p. 235.
10. Paul Reddin, *Wild West Shows* (Urbana and Chicago: University of Illinois Press, 1999), p. 128.
11. *New York Dramatic Mirror*, September 28, 1895.
12. *The Oracle*, May 28, 1892.
13. *Daily Chronicle*, London, England, June 26, 1914.
14. Elgin is a former cathedral city and Royal Burgh in Moray, Scotland.

Chapter 15

1. *Houston Daily Post*, Tuesday, October 29, 1907.
2. http://www.circushistory.org/Bandwagon/bw-1969Jan.htm.
3. Frank E. Dean, *Complete Book of Trick and Fancy Riding* (Caldwell, ID: Caxton, 1974), p. 226.
4. *The St. Louis Star*, Wednesday, October 4, 1899.
5. *Big Sandy News*, Louisa, Kentucky, October 23. 1914.
6. Paul Reddin, *Wild West Shows* (Urbana and Chicago: University of Illinois Press, 1999), p. 129.
7. *The Morning Journal*, May 20, 1894.

Chapter 16

1. *The New York Daily Tribune*, April 14, 1901.
2. *Baltimore American*, September 30, 1895.
3. *The Dispatch*, August 31, 1897.
4. *Frontier Times Magazine*, Winter 1961.

Chapter 17

1. Richard Alexis Georgian, *Cossacks, Indians and Buffalo Bill: The Adventures of Georgian Riders in America* (Naples, FL: Barringer, 2011), p. 48.
2. *The Pittsburgh Post*, Tuesday, May 2, 1893.
3. *The Pittsburgh Post*, Tuesday, May 2, 1893.
4. *The Kansas City Star*, Monday, September 11, 1893.
5. Barnum and Bailey Route Book, April 28, 1893.
6. Barnum & Bailey 1894 Program, Hertzberg Circus Museum Box 3A133, San Antonio, Texas.
7. Adam Forepaugh 1893 Route Book, Circus World Museum, Forepaugh Collection, pp. 76–78.
8. Richard Alexis Georgian, *Cossacks, Indians and Buffalo Bill: The Adventures of Georgian Riders in America* (Naples, FL: Barringer, 2011), p. 314.
9. *The New York Clipper*, May 22, 1911.
10. *Billboard*, June 10, 1911.

Chapter 18

1. Paul Reddin, *Wild West Shows* (Urbana and Chicago: University of Illinois Press, 1999), pp. 179–214.
2. Richard Alexis Georgian, *Cossacks, Indians and Buffalo Bill: The Adventures of Georgian Riders in America* (Naples, FL: Barringer, 2011), p. 402.
3. *Frontier Times Magazine*, Winter 1961, p. 5.
4. "Communist Takeover and Occupation of Georgia," United States Government Printing Office, Washington, D.C., 1955, pp. 20–21.

Bibliography

Blackstone, Sarah J. *Buckskins, Bullets & Business: A History of Buffalo Bill's Wild West*. Westport, CT: Greenwood, 1986.

Bogdanovich, Peter. *John Ford*. Oakland: University of California Press, 1978.

Bridger, Bobby. *Buffalo Bill and Sitting Bull: Inventing the Wild West*. Austin: University of Texas Press, 2002.

Collings, Ellsworth, and Alma Miller England. *The 101 Ranch*. Norman: University of Oklahoma Press, 1971.

Cunningham, Tom F. *"Your Fathers the Ghosts": Buffalo Bill's Wild West in Scotland*. Edinburgh: Black & White, 2007.

Dean, Frank E. *Complete Book of Trick and Fancy Riding*. Caldwell, ID: Caxton, 1974.

Dolidze, Giorgi. *Georgian Film—Past and Present*. Tbilisi, 1985.

Etling, K. *The Quotable Cowboy*. Guilford, CT: Lyons, 2005.

Fagen, Herb. *The Encyclopedia of Westerns*. New York: Facts on File, 2003.

Friesen, Steve. *Buffalo Bill: Scout, Showman, Visionary*. Golden, CO: Fulcrum, 2010.

Gallop, Alan. *Buffalo Bill's British Wild West*. Gloucestershire: Sutton, 2001.

Geifman, Anna. *Thou Shalt Kill: Revolutionary Terrorism in Russia, 1894–1917*. Princeton: Princeton University Press, 1993.

Georgian, Richard Alexis. *Cossacks, Indians and Buffalo Bill: The Adventures of Georgian Riders in America*. Naples, FL: Barringer, 2011.

Gipson, Fred. *Fabulous Empire: Colonel Zack Miller's Story*. Boston: Houghton Mifflin, 1946.

Hanes, Bailey C. *Bill Pickett, Bulldogger (Biography of a Black Cowboy)*. Norman: University of Oklahoma Press, 1989.

Hoberman, J. *The Dream Life: Movies, Media, and the Mythology of the Sixties*. New York: New, 2003.

Jones, Stephen F. *Socialism in Georgian Colors: The European Road to Social Democracy 1883–1917*. Cambridge, MA: Harvard University Press, 2005.

Jonnes, Jill. *Eiffel's Tower: And the World's Fair Where Buffalo Bill Beguiled, the Artists Quarreled, and Thomas Edison Became a Count*. New York: Viking Club, 2009.

Kasson, Joy S. *Buffalo Bill's Wild West: Celebrity, Memory, and Popular History*. New York: Hill and Wang, 2001.

Kitses, Jim, and Gregg Rickman, eds. *The Western Reader*. Pompton Plains, NJ: Limelight, 2004.

Koblas, John J. *The Great Cole Younger and Frank James Historical Wild West Show*. St. Cloud, MN: North Star Press of St. Cloud, 2002.

McMurtry, Larry. *The Colonel and Little Missie: Buffalo Bill, Annie Oakley, and the Beginnings of Superstardom in America*. New York: Simon and Schuster, 2006.

Munn, Michael. *John Wayne: The Man Behind the Myth*. New York: NAL, 2004.

Nakashidze, Nino. *Selected Works, Volume I*. Tbilisi, 1960.

Papashvily, George and Helen. *Anything Can Happen*. New York: Harper & Brothers, 1945.

Poole, Ernest. *The Bridge: My Own Story*. New York: Macmillan, 1940.

Posey, Jake. *Last of the Forty-Horse Drivers*. New York: Vantage, 1959.

Rattenbury, Richard C. *Arena Legacy: The Heritage of American Rodeo*. Norman: University of Oklahoma Press, 2010.

Reddin, Paul. *Wild West Shows*. Urbana and Chicago: University of Illinois Press, 1999.

Rosa, Joseph G. Robin May. *Buffalo Bill and His Wild West: A Pictorial Biography*. Lawrence: University Press of Kansas, 1989.

Russell, Don. *Wild West: A History of the Wild West Shows*. Austin: University of Texas Press, 1970.

Sagala, Sandra K. *Buffalo Bill on Stage*. Albuquerque: University of New Mexico Press, 2008.

Sidamon-Eristoff, Simon. C. *For My Grandchildren*. NP, 2002.

Slotkin, Richard. *Gunfighter Nation: Myth of the Frontier in Twentieth-Century America*. Norman: University of Oklahoma Press, 1998.

Story of the Great American West, Pleasantville, NY: Reader's Digest, 1977.

Tompkins, Jane. *West of Everything: The Inner Life of Westerns*. Oxford: Oxford University Press, 1992.

Wade, Bob. *Cowgirls*. Layton, UT: Gibbs Smith, 1995.

Walker, Janet, ed. *Westerns: Films Through History*. London: Routledge, 2001.

Walsh, Milton S. and Richard J. Salsbury. *The Making of Buffalo Bill: A Study in Heroics*. Indianapolis: Bobbs-Merrill, 1928.

Wilson, R. L. *Buffalo Bill's Wild West: An American Legend*. New York: Random House, 1998.

Index

Page numbers in **_bold italics_** indicate pages with illustrations.

Adjara 28, 36, 195*n*2
Adventures of Buffalo Bill (film) 75
Aeetes 19
Alexander II 21, 53, 61, 71
Alexander III 107, 162
Alikhanov-Avarsky, Major General 142
Altman, Robert 31
Amashukeli, Vasil 128
Amazons 19, 174
Andguladze, David 33
Antadze, Nikoloz *21*, ***85***, ***156***
Antonius Pius, Emperor 20
Anything Can Happen 23, 72, 87
Argonautika 19
Arkansas Democrat 162
Army & Navy Gazette 54
Around the Black Sea 7
Avalishvili, Konstantine 22

Bad Man of Brimstone (film) 1
Baker, Johnny 64, 123
Bakhmaro 35, 94
Bakhvi 33–4
Baramidze, Bartlome 179; broken leg 134
Baramidze, Ivane *21*, ***85***, 103, 105, ***191***; arrest 192
Barnum, P. T. 67, 185
Batumi 26–8, 32–3, 38–40, 42, 44, 82–83, 91, 97, 104, 134, 169, 185; Porto Franco 36
Beery, Wallace 1
Berliner, Emile 65
Black Coyote 29
Black Fox 170
Black Sea 17–8, 23–4, 33, 36, 54, 58, 112, 175
Blackstone, Sarah J. 42, 56, 111
Boers 69, 143
Bolkvadze, Bezhan 26
Bolsheviks 33, 128–9, 151, 154, 185, 189, 191–2
Brandt, Joseph 124
Bridge, My Own Story 134
Briggs, Harry 33
Brooklyn 68, 101, 146

Brooklyn Citizen 166, 171
Brooklyn Daily Eagle 70, 124, 146, 163
Brooklyn Sunday Citizen 107
Brown, Dee 124
Brynner, Yul 4
Buckskin Bill's troupe of Rough Riders 80
Buckskins, Bullets, and Business: The History of Wild West Show 42–3
Bud Atkinson's American Circus and Wild West Show 12
Buffalo Bill (film) 4, 31
Buffalo Bill and the Indians, or Sitting Bull's History Lesson (film) 31
Buffalo Bill Historical Center (Buffalo Bill Center of the West) 14
Buffalo Bill Museum & Grave 10
Buffalo Bill's British Wild West 196
Buffalo Bill's Wild West 4, 6, 28, 30–1, 47, 53, 58, 61, 63–5, 73, 76, 79; as educational exhibits 69; influence on cinema 75; London 39–46, 48, 51–2; program 64–5; tours 68
Buffalo Courier 155
S.S. *Buford* 8
Buntline, Ned 77, 78
Burke, Major John 46, 49, 52, 57, 67
Butler, Frank 78, 99
Byron, Lord 57, 58

Cain, W. T. 159–160
California Frank's Wild West 187
Campania 100
Campbell, Charles 144
Campbell, Colin 26
Campbell, Mary 158
Campbell Brothers' show (Campbell Bros.) 82, 144, 158
Caspian Sea 24, 36
Catlin, George 73
Caucasus 9–10, 17, 18–9, 21, 24, 34, 40–1, 44–5, 52, 54–5, 57–9, 64, 95, 107, 113, 120, 122, 142, 147, 177, 196
Chambers, James C. 32, 33
Chavchavadze, Count 22

205

Index

Chervachidze (Shervashidze), Prince 152
Chester 83
Chesterfield, Lord Philip Dormer Stanhope 172
Cheyenne Autumn (film) 30
Chibati 37, 44
Chicago 11, 74, 83, 86–91, 95, 102, 126, 150, 171–2, 180–1, 184–7, 189
Chicago Tribune 185
Chief Big Foot 30
Chief Red Fox 78
Chkhaidze, Ekaterine 90, 151
Chkhaidze, Giorgi 90, 96, *149–150*, 163
Chkhikvishvili, President Benia 140
Chkhartishvili, Konstantine 5, *8*, *21*, 179, 182
Chkhartishvili, Luka 4, *5*, *11*, *21*, 22, 38–39, 40, *41*, 57, *77*, 79, *85*, 86, *88*, 89, 92, 96, 99, 105, 113, 121, 123, 132, 157, 158–159, *161*, 166, *167–8*, 172–3, 179, 182; accident 170–1; end of career 173; fake stories 60, 160, 165; golf club 153; horsemanship 169, 171; lost photos 130–1; rivals 172; shootout at home 168
Chkhartishvili, Mikheil *22*, 87; accident 158
Chkhartishvili, Silovan 103
Chkhartishvili, Teimuraz *8*, 179, 182
Chkonia, Giorgi 87
Chkonia, Kaisar 100
Chkonia, Khariton 103, 105, 189
Chkonia, Miron *21*, 103, 105
Chkonia, Nikoloz 100–1, 127
Chkonia, Vaso 40, 174
Christus, Nymi 156
Circassia 18, 53–4, 58–9, 95
Ckhonia, David 174
Ckhonia, Irakli 40
Cleveland Plain Dealer 93
Coburn, James 4
Cody, Buffalo Bill (William Frederick Cody) 11, 15, 29, 31, 34, 54, 57, 63–78; 74; buffalo hunt 57; Congressional Medal of Honor 72; drinking problem 50; films 75; hunt with Grand Duke of Russia 71; obtained Russian Cossacks 39; Pony Express 57; Queen Victoria 42, 47, 48; riding skills of Cossacks 28; with Pawnee Bill 69, 76
Cody, Wyoming 14, 113
Cody Enterprise 14
Colchis 19
Columbus, Christopher 88
Constantinople 8, 39, 59
Cossacks 4, 6–7, 10–11, 13, 26, 28, 34, 37, 38–52, 54–8, 60–64, 69–71, 79, 86–93, 96, 100, 102–3, 107, 110–1, 113, 117–8, 120–6, 131–5, 142, 144–7, 149–151, 153–5, 157–162, 164–5, 170–6, 179, 189, 196*n*2
cowboys 6, 28, 31, 41, 45–8, 56–7, 59, 61, 64, 67, 69, 73–74, 78, 110, 113, 116, 118, 122–4, 126–7, 130–1, 143–4, 146–7, 149, 151, 158, 160, 172, 188
Cuba 63, 65, 116, 150
Cunningham, Tom F. 10, 50, 52
Curtis, William E. 7, 9, 37, 107
Czar 28, 39, 40, 57, 60, 61, 83, 120, 122, 132, 134, 135

Daily Oklahoman 81
Daily Telegraph 43
Daily Times 132
Daily Tribune 84
Darsalia, Mikha *22*
Day, Nathan C. 160
Dean, Frank E. 119, 120, 158
De Castelli, Cristoforo 20
Dgebuadze, Solomon 86
Dietreich, J. 163
Doc Carver's Wild America 73
Dolidze, Maka 174
Dolidze, Simon 174

Ebralidze, Ilarion 87, *148*, 179, 182
Ebralidze, Luka 11, 100
Eiffel's Tower and the World's Fair Where Buffalo Bill Beguiled 145
Elgin Courant & Courier 154
Eliot, Philip Frank 49
Ellis Island 72, 82, 86, 87
Engels, Friedrich 192
Ercole, C.M. 39, 41, 43, 83
Eristavi, Prince Alexander 85, 86
Eristavi (Eristoff), Prince 83, 84, 198*n*2
Escoval, Antonio 45
Europe 1, 8, 22, 30, 31, 39, 44, 53, 58, 68, 70, 73, 79, 107, 116, 122, 124, 133, 153, 173, 192, 196
Evening News Michigan 153
Evening Times 158

Fire and Sword in the Caucasus 27
Flagstaff International Film Festival 13
Ford, John 1, 2, 30, 57, 61
Forepaugh, Adam 83, 198*n*1
Fort Worth 99, 158
France 3, 39, 64, 69, 70, 90, 91, 97, 133, 175
Friesen, Steve 10
Frontier Times Magazine 172

206

Index

Gallop, Alan 10, 147
gauchos 40, 46, 47, 64, 69, 89, 96, 123
Genghis Khan 23
Georgia 1–18, 28, 33–34, 36–40, 39, 44, 50, 54–7, 61, 80–5, 87, 91–2, 94, 97–9, 99–100, 102–4, 107, 122, 128, 130, 135, 138–9, 140–2, 151–2, 159, 162–3, 173–4, 180–1, 183, 185, 189–193; annexation by Russia 7; birthplace of 17; convoy *20*, 21–22; horses 19–20; Orthodox Christians 9, 18, 108–9; Red Army 87, 190; surnames 10
Georgian, George *12*, 98, 121
Geronimo 4
Ghost Dance 28, 29, 30, 74, 75
Gigineishvili, Mose 40, *41*
Gilyarovsky, Vladimir 73
Gipson, Fred 173
Gogebashvili, Jacob 24
Gogokhia-Georgian, Alexis 10, *77*, 79, 82, 92, 96; accident 80–1; arrest 82; visited President McKinley 151
Golden Fleece 17, 19
Griffith, Goldie *94*
Guntaishvili, Melqisedek 138
Guria 6–27, 33, 44, 50–1, 56, 83, 102, 111, 153, 160, 164, 174; boycott 140; definition 24; Gurian militants *25*; Gurian republic 132–142; pirali 132, 135, 137–8; Russian Social Democratic Labour Party (RSDLP) 138, 140
Gurieli, Prince Dimitri 52, 192n14
Gvarjaladze, Giorgi 93, 100
Gvarjaladze, Sergi *22*, *114*, *141*

Hamilton Spectator 55
Heeney, George 158–9
Henry of Battenberg, Prince 49
Herald 96
Hinkle, Milton David 61
Hoberman, J. 76
Hollywood 23, 31, 131
Horn, Tom 15
Huckleberry Finn 68
Hutchinson Leader 60

Illustrated London News 44
Imereti 33, 141, 196ch3n12
Imerlishvili, Iliko 168, *169*
Imnadze (Emnadze), Barbale 121, *178*, 179, *180–1*, 182, *184*; obituary 185, *186–7*; see also Zakareishvili, Barbale
Imnadze (Emnadze), Christephore *178*, 180, 184–5

Imnadze, Iason *153*
Imnadze, Ilarion 72, *157*
Imnadze, Joseph *21*, 179
Imnadze, Karaman *21*, 179
Imnadze, Serapion 87, 111–2
Ince, Thomas 74
Indianapolis News 113, 155
Indianapolis Star 155
Indians 1, 3, 28–29, 40, 45, 47–8, 50–1, 59, 61, 63–5, 67–9, 74, 76–8, 88, 107, 110, 116–8, 124, 146–7, 149–151, 160; see also Native Americans
Irakli II, King 8
Iveria 33, 40, 44, 83, 95, 135

James, Frank 79
James, Jesse 79
Japan 69, 132–4, 147
Jason and the Argonauts 19
Jews 6, 54, 60–2, 175
Jgenti, Markoz *108*
Jibladze, Silibistro 79
Jimmie the Cossack 160
John Wayne: The Man Behind the Myth 3
Johnston, "Jeremiah Liver Eating" John 15
Jones, Buck 1
Jones Brothers show 187
Jonnes, Jill 145
Jorbenadze, Erasti 168, *169*
Jorbenadze, Ivane *21*, 103
Jorbenadze, Kirile *32*, 33
Jorbenadze, Lazare 168
Jorbenadze, Levanti 40, *41*
Jorbenadze, Sergia 179
Jordania, Noe 79, 82, 140
Jorjadze, Prince Dimitri 23

Kadjaia, Data (David) *21*, *51*, 53, 102, 103
Kalandarishvili, Giorgi 86
Kalandarishvili, Karaman 86
Kantaria, Porphile *21*
Kartvelishvili, Silovan *22*, *146*
Kasson, Joy S. 75
Kavtaradze, Teophane *21*, *94*, 121, *163*, 165, 173, 189; bar fight 162–3
Khoperia, Kirile *22*, 87, *89*, 90, *109*
Khrushchev, Nikita 2–3
Khukhunaishvili, Alexander *21*
Kikodze, Bishop of Imereti, Gabriel 33
Kikodze, Shalva 33
Kiladze, Bartlome 109
Kinloch, Alex 54
Kischko, Glenn (Shorty) 69

207

Index

Kit Carson's Buffalo Ranch Wild West 61, 159
Kobaladze, Michael 83
Kotkoshvili, M. T. 95
Kutaisi 20, 22, 39, 57, 134, 141
Kvali 165
Kvitaishvili, Kaisar **8**, 98, 180, 189, ***190***
Kvitaishvili, Kitilia ***178***, ***180***
Kvitaishvili, Maro 128–9, ***178***, 179, 182, 183; *see also* Zakareishvili, Maro
Kvitaishvili, Petre 98
Kvitaishvili, Ushangi **21**, **85**, 103
Kvitaishvili, Veliko 121, 128–9, 167, ***177–8***, 179, ***180***, 182, ***183–4***, 185, ***186***

Labladzi, Michael 83
Lanchkhuti 10, 14, 33, 37, 39, 44, 56, 93, 97–8, 100, 168, 173
Lang, David Marshall 18
Lazarenko 142
Lenin 12
Letters to His Son 172
Lexington News 79
Lincoln State Journal 111
Lodge, Henry Cabot 46
Lomadze, Jimshet **99**, 109
London Serio-Comic Journal 45
London Start 112
S.S. *La Lorraine* 87
Lucania 147
Lucretia 72
Lyons, Roland 11

Magnificent Seven (film) 3
Makharadze, Alexandre 34
Makharadze, Ivane 11, 33, 34, **35**, 37, 39, 40, **41**, 42, 48, 50, 55, 85, 86, 112, 151, 162, 192; visit to Savage Club 151
Makharadze, Ivane "Kid" 86
Makharadze, Pavle **21**, 34, **81**, 103, 118, **146**, 192
Makharadze, Qishvard 86
Makharadze, Silibistro 34, 86; murder 138
Man Who Shot Liberty Valance (film) 57
Maqsimenishvili, Giorgi 83
Marx, Karl 141, 192
Matitashvili, Gaston 83
Maynard, Ken 1
Mazeppa 45, 57, 58, 59
McMurtry, Larry 46
McNeill, Major General Sir John C. 47
McQueen, Steve 4
Menagarishvili, Nestor ***115***

Metekhi prison 168
Mexicans 45, 46, 48, 57, 64, 67, 74, 110, 118, 122, 143, 146, 160
Mgaloblishvili, Dimitri 40, **41**, 84, 93, 159, 174; fight 175
Mgaloblishvili, Frida 38, 83, 84, 86, 108, 123, 143, 174–5, 178; accident 179; interview 176–7; Roman riding 178; visited President Cleveland 151
Mgaloblishvili, Giorgi 174
Mikaberidze, Kote 128, ***129***
Miller, Zack 173
Miller Brothers 101; Ranch Wild West Show 74, 151, 166, 168, 173, 189
Mingrelia 24, 55, 58, 141
Minneapolis Times 175
Mizuno, George 134
Mogzauri 141
S.S. *Mohawk* 52
Monday Morning 89
Morning Journal 165, 176
Moskovskie Vedomosti 51, 54
Mshvidobadze, Bartlome 87, ***136***
Mshvidobadze, Ioram **22**, 100
Mshvidobadze, Joseph ***103***, 104, 179
Mshvidobadze, Kvirosi 104, ***106***
Mshvidobadze, Laphier 100
Munn, Michael 3
Murvan ibn Muhamad 24
Murvanidze, Alexander **81**, 105
Murvanidze, Ephrasina 98
Murvanidze, Platon **8**, 98
Mutiny in Guria (film) 131

Nakaidze, Cio (Shio) 107, 162
Nakashidze, Nino 92, 112, 128
Napoleonic wars 43
Nasakirali 142
National Geographic 4
Native Americans 30–1, 56–7, 73, ***145***; *see also* Indians
Nelson, General Miles 29
New Times 82
New York 9, 14, 36, 40, 53, 65, 68, 73, 79, 84, 86, 90, 100–3, 116, 124, 126, 129, 133, 146–7, 149, 155, 176, 182, 185, 192–3
New York Clipper 103, 164
New York Times 55, 61, 103, 149
New York Tribune 100
Newcastle Guardian 147
S.S. *Niagara* 98
Nobel Company 33
Nuttal, Aron 10

208

Index

Oakley, Annie 64, 68, 74, 76, 78, 99, 147
Odessa 17, 39, 100, 169
O'Hara, Maureen 4
Okhranka (secret police) 82
Oliver, Thomas 28, 32, 33, 34, 37, *41*, 57, 63
Oracle 40
Oragvelidze, Simon *21*, *81*, 103, *146*
Ozurgeti 33, 39, 57, 101, 174

Papashvily, George 22, 72, 87
Paris 39, 54, 84, 88, 90, 103, 123, 175–6
Parsman, King of Iberia 20, 21
Pataraia, Khalampri *159*, 160, 179, 182; murder 159–160
Pataraia, Zosime 174
Pawnee Bill (Major Gordon W. Lillie) 4, 60, 69, 75–6, 123, 132, 151, 153, 162, 166, 182
Pen and Pencil 55
Peter the Great 58
Petite Journal 83
Philadelphia Inquirer 122
Pictorial World 43
Pirtskhalaishvili, Kirile *22*, *43*, *137*, *178*, 184
Pittsburg Dispatch 84
Pittsburgh Post 83
Platoff, Count 43
Ponsonby, General Sir Henry 47
Poole, Ernest 134
Princequillo 23
Princess Beatrice 48, 49
Prometheus 19

Queen Victoria 42, 47–52, 48, 50, 51

Radamist 20
Raikini, Charles 83
Ramishvili, Noe 140
Rattenbury, Richard C. 127
Read, Opie 70
Remington, Frederic 40, 118, 123, 124
Rhodios, Apollonius 19
Riders of the Wild West (book) 13
Riders of the Wild West (film) 13
Ringling Bros. 34, 180, 18, 189
Robakidze, Grigol 24
Robin Hood 138
Rockefeller, John D. 33
Roosevelt, Franklin 2
Roosevelt, Theodore 46, 65, 116, 124, *149*, 150
Rough Riders 11, 31, 39, 46, 49, 52, 63–4, 80, 84, 87–9, 95, 107, 119, 122, 124, 143
Russia 3–4, 6–7, 22, 34, 53–4, 58, 60, 85, 108, 128, 131–4, 141, 151, 190

Saint Louis Daily Globe Democrat 153
Saint Paul Pioneer Press 157
St. Petersburg 41, 60, 73, 128, 165
Sakhokia, Tedo 54
Salsbury, Nate 31, 40, 41, 47, 48, 49, 50, 67, 150
San Francisco Chronicle 94
San Francisco Examiner 183
Saturday Review 54
Saturday Times 170
Schamyl 58–9
Schultz, Frank 163
Sergia, Sam 98
Shakarishvili, Parnaoz *22*
Shalikashvili, General John 1
Shevardnadze, Datiko 138
Shevardnadze, Dimitri 33
Shevardnadze, Eduard 138
Shimp, Robert 14
Sidamon-Eristavi, Simon 87
Sitting Bull 28–29
Slack, John 126
Society Circus 95
Sovetsky Ekran 129
Spragg, Susan 45
Stagecoach (film) 1
Stalin, Joseph 2–3, 12, 79, 107
Star 37, 55
Stradizi, Lewis 83
Stravinsky, Igor 26
Surguladze, Nikoloz *5*, 11, 13, *22*, 103, *139*
Sutherland, Ed 145
Sweeney, William 147

Talakhadze, Joseph 86
Tarasov 134
Tarsaidze, Alexandre 85
Tarzan (film) 3
Tbilisi 1, 2, 6, 10, 12–3, 22, 27, 34, 40, 79, 90, 98, 128, 130, 134, 168
Tericuly, Andrew 83
Times 28
Tom Mix Museum 113
Tompkins Wild West show 187
Trail of a Falcon (film) 3
trick riders 4, 6, 7, 9, 10, 13, 15, 37, 62, 73, 80, 83, 84, 89, 90–2, 110–1, 118–121, 126, 128, 129, 131, 138, 140, 158, 182, 192, 193; accidents 100–2, 158–160; affairs and fe-

Index

male admirers 153–4; appetite 110; diary of unknown rider 17, 54, 65, 70, 76, 93, 106, 117–8, 145, 150, 171; dzhigitovka 120; fake medals 59, 162; fights 143, 145–6, 160–2; French Foreign Legion 90; horses 112; influence on cowboys 124–7; language barrier 102, 143; "Londoner" 92, 102, 122; nicknames 159; saddle 113; Siberia 132, 142, 165, 192; stolen apples 163–4; strike 103; suicide 154, 168, 192; Windsor 47, 49, 51
Tsamtsishvili, Academician Amiran 28, 180
Tsetskhladze, Joseph 99, *126*
Tsintsadze, Alexander 83, 100–2, 119
Tsintsadze, Besarion 40, *41*
Tsintsadze (Nodia), Christine 179, 182–3
Tsintsadze, Dimitri *22, 75, 101,* 104
Tsintsadze, Ese *22*
Tsintsadze, Ilarion 179
Tsintsadze, Irakli *21*; death 158–9
Tsintsadze, Kirile *180*
Tsintsadze, Meliton 40, *41*, 100–2
Tsintsadze, Nikoloz 103
Tsintsadze, Panteleimon 56, *59*, 100, 102, 131
Tsintsadze, Polta 155
Tskvitishvili, Alexander *37*
Tsnobis Purtsely 63, 92, 99, 166, 172
Tsuladze, Onophre *8, 96,* 97, 99
Tsuladze, Vaso (Sam Sergie) *97–8*, 105, 180; Sam's Club 99
Tsutsunava, Alexander 128–131
Turchaninoff, Ivan 86
Turner, Frederick Jackson 74
Tvaladze, Raphiel 83
Twain, Mark 68

Uratadze, Grigol 140
Urushadze, Islam 105

Vachnadze, Nato 128
Villari, Luigi 27, 140

Wade, Bob 126
Walsh, Richard J. 144
Washington Post 132, 155
Washtenaw Times 63
Wayne, John 1, 2, 3
Weekly Dispatch 40
Weissmuller, Johnny 3
Wellman, William 4
western movies 1, 3, 31, 75, 76, 128
Who's Guilty? (film) 128, *129, 130*
Who's Guilty? (play) 92, 112, 128
Wild West shows 13, 34, 49, 61, 67, 74, 79–80, 97, 105, 127, 132, 150, 155, 172, 189–190
Winchester, Juti 14
Wolf Ticket 79, 198n1
Woodrow Wilson 150
Wounded Knee massacre 29, 30, 31
Wovoka 28

Younger, Cole 79

Zakareishvili, Barbale 179–180, 184; *see also* Imnadze (Emnadze), Barbale
Zakareishvili, Maro 120, 179; *see also* Kvitaishvili, Maro
Zascetely (Tsereteli), Archil 187
Zascetely (Tsereteli), Babilina 187–8
Zilitzi, Samuel 83
Zurabeg 72

www.ingramcontent.com/pod-product-compliance
Ingram Content Group UK Ltd.
Pitfield, Milton Keynes, MK11 3LW, UK
UKHW041959140426
5217IPUK00015B/884